Wanna Buy Some Rocks?

The Journey of a Stay-at-Home Dad

By Jim Renaud

This book is dedicated to my beautiful wife Michele

and my two incredible kids, Ryan and Danielle.

Without their inspiration and support,

I could not have written this book.

Preface

I am a firm believer that there is nothing funnier or more inspiring than real life. Movies, plays, and television shows have all tried to capture this with their comedies and dramas. Stand-up comics have always tried to make us laugh. I love laughing as well as being inspired, so I am always being drawn to those types of shows and productions. In my entire life, I have always sought out the best. Based on my experience, living life provides the most amazing moments of pure joy, laughter, and awe. My journey as a stay-at-home dad has had many of those moments. I hope that you laugh or you find some inspiration as you read about my journey...

Table of Contents

Table of Contents - cont.

Chapter 1

How It All Started

A Little Background

Before commencing, a little background is needed. I graduated from college in 1985 with an undergraduate degree in Civil Engineering from the University of Delaware. Upon graduation, marriage was right around the corner and I received only one job offer from General Dynamics in Connecticut. Knowing that the bills needed to be paid, I took the job and Michele and I were soon settled into our small apartment in New London.

Initially my job was in a training program for the testing of nuclear reactors on submarines for about a year, and then I decided that the work was not a good fit for me professionally. Therefore, I went out into the job market and tried to find work in the transportation field somewhere farther south. Fortunately there was a position in Valley Forge, Pennsylvania, working for a small consulting firm that provided a number of services including the development of traffic studies. It was good work that provided me with lots of opportunity. The motto was, "If you were up to the responsibility, then you got it!"

I was there for several years when my boss came up to me and said he wanted to start up his own consulting firm. He wanted me to come along, and after some consideration, I said yes. It was a real challenge to start up a new business from scratch. They say that the first two years are very challenging and a lot of firms fail. Well they were right, and I surely did not want to be a failure. There were many long days and nights making sure the deadlines were met and new work kept coming in. It was rewarding work but very time-consuming.

The climate at the firm got ugly when one partner decided to buy the other partner out. The situation went to court and ... well let's say it was not a fun time. My wife Michele suggested in October of that year that we move back to Maryland. (Between the two of us, she has always been the spontaneous one). I began to interview and once again was very fortunate and found a new job with another consulting firm. By December of that same year I had moved to Maryland. Michele and our four-year-old son Ryan followed me there three months later. It was my hope that I would be there until the end of my career. The firm was well-established, and the demands placed on me were a bit more realistic and comfortable than they had been previously. I stayed with that firm for about ten years. I was somewhat disillusioned and realized that a change was needed. I had numerous ideas that would allow the company to be more productive, but my ideas went nowhere.

Coming to a Crossroads

So what did I do? I took off three days to pray and reflect about my situation and develop a plan. It was actually a pivotal point in my life. Some goals were developed and there were thoughts about what my dreams were and how I could go about achieving them. My list of goals and dreams included the following:

- ✓ Live long enough to see my grandchildren
- ✓ Enjoy our new house (instead of just working on it)
- ✓ Develop a plan to enjoy my senior years with Michele
- ✓ Keep long-time friends and develop new ones
- ✓ Develop a healthier outlook on life
- ✓ Work on my hobbies more
- ✓ Become a muscle car magazine expert

Brainstorming

I then brainstormed various vocation options. I pulled out all the stops and even considered dream jobs developed in my earlier years. Of course, there were the conservative options like staying at my current job or going to another firm or municipality and doing the same type of work. But I also considered teaching, writing, opening a restaurant, or becoming a car mechanic. I have enjoyed working with my hands and wood, so there were the handyman, carpentry, and woodworking businesses to consider. I considered opening a hobby/collectible shop, and then there was the used car magazine dealer business.

The list of possibilities did not stop there. Working for the Boy Scouts has always interested me since it is a program that I believe in strongly. I also enjoyed building models, so becoming a professional model builder intrigued me. Working for the National Park Service would tie into my love for the great outdoors and, of course, there was my love of architecture. I had wanted to be an architect back in high school, but my guidance counselor informed me that the only opportunities came about if an architect were to die or retire. I am no expert, but that did not sound like a good prospect to me.

I was full of ideas! I also considered being an office organizer since one of my strengths is organization and space relationships. Finally, quitting altogether and becoming a stay-at-home dad was considered. However, I admit that this was one of my least seriously-considered options. Being an engineer, I went about my evaluation of each of my brainstormed ideas in a very logical way.

The Evaluation Stage

I first evaluated our financial needs, both short-term and long-term, and looked at our savings situation. Then the pros and cons of each alternative were weighed. The option for quitting had several pros including taking pressure off of Michele by picking up some of her responsibilities around the house, saving money by doing some of the work that we had hired others to do, doing more volunteer work, catching up on some projects around the house, and most importantly, being more involved with our kids' lives.

However, I considered there to be a number of drawbacks to staying home. I would have no benefits, the long-term goals of the kids going to college would be impaired, and our daughter Danielle's wedding and our retirement would suffer. It would put a strain on being able to pay the regular bills. Financial emergencies like the heat pump dying would be harder to address. And of course, many of the perks in our current lifestyle like big vacations, eating out, going to professional sports events, would have to go away. I really did not like the feel of this particular alternative. It seemed to me to be a bit irresponsible.

I decided that the best course of action was to stay at my current job and to really try to address my concerns and take the steps needed to make my working experience a pleasant one. The next step in my plan was to reassess the situation after a year and if the issues had not been resolved, I would then go onto work for another local firm or municipality. Overall, I wanted to work long enough to meet some of the larger financial goals like putting the kids through college, but I knew that I wanted to pursue something else eventually. And so part of my plan was to cultivate other career possibilities once I was ready to retire from a civil engineering career as well as pursue hobbies that met my needs. The plan was fair to me and my family and I was quite proud of it. I felt that the hand of God had really played a part in the development of this plan.

Presenting my Plan to Michele

I presented the plan to Michele when we were in our minivan one day. I will never forget making my presentation to her. You see, I was quite proud of all of my efforts, and I thought it was well thought out and complete.

After making my presentation, I asked Michele for her thoughts and she surprised me by asking me if I had thought about quitting and becoming a stay-at-home dad. I told her that I did consider it, but that I thought it was financially not a good idea. She said she would take a look at the numbers and see if we could get by for a while. After her assessment, she recommended we take the plunge and have me become a stay-at-home dad. So that's where it all began. Once again my spontaneous wife lives up to her reputation!

Chapter 2

Grocery Shopping

Shortly after I quit my job, I learned of many chores and errands that would become my responsibility. One of them was grocery shopping. Now, I am not your typical guy and I actually like to shop. I remember when Michele and I were a young married couple and we would go grocery shopping together. Michele would be very task-oriented and would try to get the shopping done as quickly as possible. I, on the other hand, would casually go up and down the aisles looking at various non-needed products just taking my good old time. My approach created some tension in our relationship, but it goes to show you our different mindsets.

Some Early Tests Utilizing my Engineering Know-how

Preparing for and executing the grocery shopping adventure allowed me to use many of my engineering skills to their utmost. First, I had to be able to think on my feet and communicate clearly. It appears that I was responsible to know how much of every product we had in the house at any given time. Case in point: It seemed that the kids were always asking if I had gotten them the shampoo or whatever they were running out of. I would respond to their question with another question and ask if they had put it on the grocery list. When they replied, "No," I would say that I did not get them their shampoo. It was that simple. In reality, I would go through the entire pantry, refrigerator, freezer and various closets before setting out to shop so I would (hopefully) successfully re-stock our house. However, I am not perfect so they learned quickly to put the items they wanted on the list!

And then there were the coupons! I needed to be organized and diligent to keep up with these pesky buggers. Our metropolitan newspaper along with the local paper would have several coupon inserts consisting of about twenty pages each. I would spend an hour or so wading through to see if there were any coupons associated with products that we needed. After clipping out the coupons, I would put them into the coupon organizer. The organizer is set up into individual files by product. If there were multiple coupons dealing with any one given product, which was usually the case, then I would organize them by chronological order according to their expiration date.

After the shopping list was created, I would cross-reference it with the coupons I had clipped to see if there were any that could be used. Of course, I would be checking the expiration dates on the coupons to make sure they were still valid and throw out any that had expired. I would then mark the items on the shopping list that I had a coupon for so I would know when I got to the store. You might be asking, "Why did I need to know all of this?" The answer is quite simple. When I got to the point where I was looking for that specific item in the store, I would have the coupon in my hand since the coupon would let me know what criteria I had to meet.

Trying to Make Sense (& Cents!) of Coupons

For those of you who have never used a coupon, let me explain. The coupons usually have a quantity criteria. In other words, I would have to buy twenty-four rolls of toilet paper or six boxes of pancake mix in order to get the dollar off. To make matters more complicated, my grocery store would have double coupons, but only if it had a face value of less than one dollar. In addition, the store would sometimes have coupons that would triple a coupon's value, but again, only in certain instances. Wait, it gets worse! I cannot tell you how many times I would find myself staring at a product made by two manufacturers trying to figure out which one was cheaper after the coupons and any special promotions were taken into consideration. By the time I got to this point, I would simply give up and just use the coupon!

I then started memorizing the layout of the store. I would set up my list so that it coincided with Aisle 1, followed by Aisle 2, and so forth. I would organize the coupons I brought with me in the same fashion. I would be one very organized person, so you can imagine my chagrin when they would reorganize some part of the store or move one product from here over to there. I would be out of sorts for a couple of weeks until my mind could acclimate to the new layout. It still amazes me how my mind craves a constant environment!

<u>Way Too Many Choices</u>

Speaking of consistency, I have to address that issue right here. You know how they say, "Some things will never change?" Well, they are not talking about the number of choices we have in this country. It is my opinion that we have too many choices. It really becomes overwhelming!
I will use toothpaste as an example. You would think this would be easy, right? Oh no -- not by a long shot!

I remember as a kid that there were <u>two</u> choices when it came to toothpaste at our local grocery store. There was Colgate and there was Crest. I think my memory is serving me correct since I remember when Sensodyne came out, and my mom was thrilled because she had sensitive teeth. That made three choices. Well now the choices are almost unlimited.

Let's just take Crest toothpaste alone: There is Pro Health that comes in four different flavors – Clean Mint, Clean Cinnamon, Clean Night Mint, and Fresh Clean Mint with Whitening. There is Whitening with Scope Extreme, Extra White with Scope, and let's not forget Whitening Plus Scope which comes in three different flavors – Minty Fresh Striped, Cool Peppermint, and Citrus Splash. Then there is

Whitening Expressions that comes in Winter Green Ice, Extreme Herbal Mint, Cinnamon Rush, and Refreshing Vanilla Mint. Nature's Expressions is a Pure Peppermint Fresh flavor, and the Extra Whitening comes in Clean Mint. The Multi-care Whitening is a Fresh Mint flavor (mint is very popular) and who can forget the Tartar Protection? There is also a Cavity Protection variety as well as the kids' toothpaste.

For some reason, there is also a variety of packaging options with the toothpaste. There is your old school tube that you simply squeeze and then there is a pump action dispenser. Some are packaged in containers with a celebrity on the front while others feature a popular children's product. Most flavors and types come in one of three sizes. The size choices are 4.2 ounces, 6.0 ounces and 7.8 ounces. There were close to seventy different options to choose from and that is only the Crest brand! That's right! This list excludes all of the varieties of other toothpaste brands like Aim, Colgate's Close-Up and Ultra Brite, Pepsodent, Listerine, Arm and Hammer, Sensodyne, Biotene, Aquafresh, and Rembrandt that I saw on the shelves!! There was half an aisle dedicated to just toothpaste. The first time I tried to focus on buying a tube of toothpaste I thought my head was going to explode. Now I just buy what the coupon is for.

My Ruminations at the Check-out Line

Checking out is one of my favorite parts of the grocery shopping process. I will have a certain air of pride about me as I approach the cashier who will soon find out how efficiently I shopped. Then there are the tabloids all sitting there waiting to have their front pages read. I find myself being drawn to them like a mosquito is drawn to a bug light. I cannot wait to find out the latest details of what wacky occurrences are going on in celebrities' lives. I am always curious as to why only certain stars are featured in all of these magazines. Are they the only ones with anything newsworthy going on in their lives? Could it be that they enjoy the attention? Is it possible that they do not know that it is feasible to try and live a life that is not documented every second of every day? I am not sure, but I will bet you they do not use coupons when they go grocery shopping or even grocery shop at all …

Chapter 3

Get on it

Add Acid to acid loving plants
Rotate back yard decorative flags
Repair driveway lights (again)
Cavlk things
Mantain the car(s)
Fix any thing that breaks
Trim cat's toenails
Trubleshoot computer (ugh!)
Clean dehumidifier filters
Undecorate house from holidays

Where to Begin?

One of my first tasks when I became Mr. Mom[1] was to catch up on all that needed to be done around the house. I believe that everyone who owns a house experiences the anxiety of getting it all done. In addition, we all understand the mundane tasks that don't even get noticed but are still necessary. Keeping up with a house is a daunting and sometimes thankless task. On one of the morning television talk shows, it was mentioned the amount of money saved by one parent staying at home. That was inspiration for me!

Blame it on the fact that I am a Civil Engineer, but I had to develop a plan. Actually, the plan developed me. Initially, there were three things I knew I had to do on a regular basis.

[1] "*Mr. Mom*" is an MGM movie from 1983

They were:

1. Cut the lawn
2. Grocery shop
3. Clean the house

Before I became a stay-at-home dad, I was primarily responsible for the outside of the house and the maintenance of our vehicles. I soon realized that the outdoor work required much more than cutting the lawn.

Additional tasks included:

- ✓ Spray bushes for bugs
- ✓ Set up Japanese Beetle bags
- ✓ Remove wasp nests
- ✓ Add acid to the acid loving plants
- ✓ Spray or remove weeds
- ✓ Create plant beds
- ✓ Plant plants
- ✓ Hook up outdoor sound system
- ✓ Tear down the outdoor sound system
- ✓ Rotate front yard decorative flags
- ✓ Rotate back yard decorative flags
- ✓ Wax Patio furniture
- ✓ Set up patio/deck/bar furniture
- ✓ Tear down patio/deck/bar furniture
- ✓ Constantly repair tiki torches
- ✓ Set up fake plants (which Michele does not even like!! That's another story ...)
- ✓ Tear down fake plants (see above)
- ✓ Drain hot tub
- ✓ Clean hot tub filters
- ✓ Water hanging plants
- ✓ Mulch beds

- ✓ Constantly repair driveway lights
- ✓ Caulk driveway cracks
- ✓ Caulk anything (I like to caulk)
- ✓ Fix picnic table
- ✓ Build retaining walls
- ✓ Build steps
- ✓ Build patio
- ✓ Build patio bars
- ✓ Build fire pit
- ✓ Take trash up for collection
- ✓ Bring empty trash containers back
- ✓ Take recycle items up for collection
- ✓ Bring empty recycling containers back
- ✓ Replace light bulbs
- ✓ Fix hoses
- ✓ Place soil
- ✓ Plant grass
- ✓ Fertilize lawn
- ✓ Collect sticks off of lawn
- ✓ Cut grass
- ✓ Trim bushes
- ✓ Edge gardens
- ✓ Rake grass clippings
- ✓ Sweep grass clippings
- ✓ Rake leaves
- ✓ Clear leaves from gutters
- ✓ Sweep leaves off of roof
- ✓ Shovel snow off of driveway
- ✓ Set up outdoor decorations
- ✓ Take down outdoor decorations
- ✓ Split firewood

- ✓ Stack firewood
- ✓ Bring firewood into house
- ✓ Maintain bicycles
- ✓ Take fleet of cars out for maintenance
- ✓ Take fleet of cars out for emissions inspection
- ✓ Wash cars
- ✓ Wax cars
- ✓ Clean interior of cars
- ✓ Top off fluids in cars
- ✓ Maintain air pressure in car tires
- ✓ Run cars to top of the driveway whenever there is the threat of snow
- ✓ Maintain lawnmower
- ✓ Maintain weed whacker
- ✓ Maintain blower
- ✓ Paint trim work
- ✓ Paint front door
- ✓ Paint basketball pole
- ✓ Paint septic tank lid
- ✓ Paint shutters
- ✓ Power wash house
- ✓ Power wash and seal front walk

Finding Ways to be Wiser

It was clear that we needed a person full -time working on the outdoor and car maintenance items. Some of the things I have done over the years are truly insane. For instance, I keep installing new plant beds. I think we are up to over twenty beds. I have twenty cubic yards of mulch delivered each spring, and it takes me about forty hours to mulch the beds. Another crazy thing I do is have the lawn fertilized. This makes the grass grow faster and extends our growing season, creating more and more work for me. I now start cutting the grass in March and don't stop until November.

One smart thing I did was hire someone else to do the fertilizing. I did the math and determined it costs me as much to do it myself as to hire others to do it. I figured that my approach will allow me to have more energy to cut the lawn. The other lawn care task that drives me batty is raking the leaves. They start to fall in August and don't stop until January. I figured I rake the lawn eight times per year and it takes up to eight hours just to rake the lawn once. I haul up to thirty tarp-loads of leaves into the woods on any one given weekend. A word to the wise: Don't buy a wooded lot!

This picture does not do the amount of leaves justice!

And Now, Tackling the Inside of the House

The inside was no less intimidating. I sat down and figured out what needed to be done:

- ✓ Fold Laundry
- ✓ Cook

- ✓ Wash dishes
- ✓ Run dishwasher
- ✓ Empty dishwasher
- ✓ Vacuum rugs
- ✓ Dust Rooms
- ✓ Scrub tile floors
- ✓ Clean bathrooms
- ✓ Collect trash in house
- ✓ Water plants
- ✓ Change the cat's litter
- ✓ Trim the cat's toenails
- ✓ Brush the cat
- ✓ Give the cat medicine
- ✓ Replace light bulbs
- ✓ Snake toilets
- ✓ Build floors in attic spaces
- ✓ Paint rooms
- ✓ Caulk anything (I *really* like to caulk ... have I mentioned this before?)
- ✓ Adjust door locks as necessary
- ✓ Clean windows
- ✓ Wrap presents
- ✓ Hook up televisions, VCRs, DVDs, game systems
- ✓ Trouble shoot cable issues
- ✓ Hook up stereos
- ✓ Hook up computers
- ✓ Troubleshoot computer issues
- ✓ Hook up phones
- ✓ Frame pictures
- ✓ Hang blinds
- ✓ Hang curtains

- ✓ Clean VCR heads
- ✓ Clean tape deck heads
- ✓ Put house fan cover on in the fall
- ✓ Take house fan cover off in the spring
- ✓ Shut down hose bibs in fall
- ✓ Open hose bibs in the spring
- ✓ Replace filters in the two circulators
- ✓ Replace the filter in the humidifier
- ✓ Clean the filters in the dehumidifiers
- ✓ Replace the house water filter
- ✓ Replace the filter in the sink purifier
- ✓ Decorate house for holidays
- ✓ Un-decorate house from holidays
- ✓ Assemble anything that needs assembly
- ✓ Understand any new equipment that comes into the house
- ✓ Fix *anything* that breaks

Reaching a Similar Conclusion

Once again, it was clear that we needed a person full-time working on the indoor tasks. Just setting up and understanding all of the new "stuff" that comes in through our front door is intimidating. There are cameras, cell phones, cars, toys, watches, televisions, DVDs, stereos, computers (hardware and software), game systems, phones (yes, we still have a land line), furniture, watches, appliances, cable, exercise equipment, laptops, vacuums, tools, heating equipment, etc. I love it when you get a simple piece of equipment, like a toaster and it comes with a forty-page owner's manual. Give me a break! It's just a toaster! Unfortunately, I am one of those people who actually reads the owner's manual.

Finally, there is the administrative side to the job of keeping the household up and running. The following are some of the facets of the job:

- ✓ Set up vacations and trips
- ✓ Set up yearly calendar
- ✓ Purchase presents
- ✓ Wrap Presents
- ✓ Make photo albums
- ✓ Go through mail
- ✓ Pay bills
- ✓ Set up and send Christmas cards
- ✓ Call for any services (Chimney sweep, UV filter light bulb, oil service, deck power wash and seal, driveway sealing, tree maintenance, pest control, septic tank pump down)
- ✓ Answer the phone
- ✓ Check and respond to emails
- ✓ Check and respond to voice mail
- ✓ Place orders
- ✓ Filing
- ✓ Taxes
- ✓ Write letters
- ✓ Paperwork
- ✓ Clip coupons
- ✓ Send birthday and anniversary cards
- ✓ Maintain/update computer
- ✓ Prepare for parties and visits

The biggest facet of the administrative side of things was the paperwork. It was so big that it warranted its own chapter (as you will soon find out). The thing I need to mention is the filing associated with all of this paperwork. We have six drawers of files covering everything from insurance to doctors and also household projects, banking, professional organizations, taxes, utilities, school, Christmas, church, vacations, kids' activities, clubs, investments, mortgage, etc. The list goes on and on. One of the first tasks I tried to tackle was to go through our files, weed out the outdated information, and make it more organized. It took me two years. Obviously, we need someone full-time on just the administrative duties that need to be done around our house!

Disclaimer: *It was pointed out during the editing done by my wife that some of the above listed tasks were done before I became a stay-at-home dad. This is true. In addition, it was pointed out that I may not be the primary person responsible for a given task. This is true, although I do help with each of these tasks. The point that I was trying to make is that when all of it is considered, it is clear that it takes a tremendous amount of effort to do all you are supposed to do to keep a household afloat!*

Chapter 4

Clothing is Optional

A Little Bit of Heaven

Many of my behaviors changed soon after I began my journey as a stay-at-home dad. Not only did I begin to do all of the household projects that we had been putting off for years, but I let my hair grow. I began to wear cheap bracelets. I grew a goatee. I began to dress as a slob. I was becoming a hippie. All of this happened in stages, especially the dressing behavior.

First, I realized that I could simply slip on my jeans over my pajamas and jump right into my day. At the end of the day, I would simply slip off my jeans and be ready to go to bed whenever I pleased. In my old life in the mornings, I would change out of my pajamas, put on my business attire, and go to work. When I got home from work, I would change into more comfortable clothes, and later I would change back into my pajamas for bed. This new routine was much quicker and more efficient. I was in heaven!

Sometimes my brainstorming went to the next step, and I would simply wear my pajamas all day long as long as I wasn't going out to run errands or attend a meeting. I mean, who cared what clothes I had on while I planned that year's Boy Scout Summer Camp experience or while I was cleaning the upstairs toilet? Darn it--I could wear anything I wanted, and nobody was going to stop me!

I find that I can wear my bathrobe all day!

Chapter 5

Making a Difference

The Amazing Boy Scout Program

Sometimes we get an opportunity to participate in something fabulous; something that gives us a sense of purpose; something that we know is making the world a better place and truly making a positive difference in the lives of others. That's the way I feel when I reflect on my participation in the Boy Scout program. Scouting is an incredible organization. I believe it is one of the best in the world. It is the only organization that provides such a wide range of experiences for young boys developing into young men.

Array of Merit Badges

Merit badges, for example, offer the boys the opportunity to do something new or to learn more about something they enjoy. The merit badges cover topics ranging from Bird Study to Nuclear Science. The Scouting program involves numerous outdoor activities including camping, hiking, orienteering, hiking, biking, canoeing, white water rafting, rowing, using the rifle, archery, rock climbing, caving, skiing, kayaking, fishing, and water sports, just to name a few.

By participating in the Scouting program, the boys have the chance to see some of the most beautiful sights that Mother Nature has to offer in our region. Our troop experienced the ponies on Assateague Island, the incredible views from the Appalachian Trail and Camelback Mountain, the adventure of white water rafting along the Lehigh and Youghiogheny Rivers, and biking through St. Michaels along the Chesapeake & Ohio (C&O) Canal Trail. The boys learn how to become good citizens in their community, nation and even on a world-wide scale. They learn first aid skills and how to stay physically fit. They learn what to do in an all types of emergencies and how their environment works. They learn how to manage their personal life and what it means to be a positive member of their families. Scouts are always doing service in the community and trying to make the world a better place by volunteering their time.

Building Leadership

The most incredible part of the Scouting program to me is the opportunity the boys have to lead others. As the boys get older, they take on various leadership positions. With some guidance from the older scouts and the adults, they learn what it takes to be a good leader and then they apply what they've learned.

In an ideal situation, the troop is truly "boy-led." This means that it would be completely up to the troop's Senior Patrol Leader, along with his Assistant Senior Patrol Leader and other Patrol Leaders, to determine what the troop will be doing at the weekly meetings and on the weekend trips. The Senior Patrol Leader delegates responsibilities, oversees the workings of the troop, and learns how to motivate others. The older boys work with the younger boys in developing their basic Scouting skills and in leading them. The older boys become role models for the younger ones and, if things go well, the pattern then continues as the younger boys mature and become the older boys.

Added Benefit of Close Friendships

The boys, as well as the adults, develop strong friendships. This is probably due to the uniqueness of their Scouting experiences. For example, I do not believe that many kids go to school on Monday and talk about how they biked fifty miles that weekend, rappelled down a 100-foot high stone wall, or led a group of forty-five boys during a "Camporee" event.

When I have asked the boys in my son's troop what they most enjoy about it, nine times out of ten they have said it is the friendships they've made with the other boys in the troop. They look forward to spending time with each other and experiencing new and exciting events together. The adults also enjoy developing new friendships. The troop's Scoutmaster and I have become very close friends over the past eight years that we have worked together. We have not only done scout stuff together, but we have also attended car shows and helped each other complete projects around our houses. Our friendship is something I truly value.

Enjoying the friendships I've made in Scouting

Values & Achievement

Speaking of values, the Boy Scouts program has a very strong foundation of values at its core. In fact, I believe that they are so strong that it is impossible to meet them all. I encourage the scouts in our troop to strive to meet all of them, but I realize that the boys will each have their own weaknesses. The values promote that the boys do their best, to be true to their God, to do their duty to their country, to help others, to always be prepared, to stay physically fit, to actively participate in things going on around them, and to stick to good morals. And then there are the Scout Laws.

These laws are that the scouts are to be trustworthy, loyal, helpful, friendly, courteous, kind, obedient, cheerful, thrifty, brave, clean, and reverent. That is a tall order!

Everyone gets to experience a sense of real accomplishment, whether it is completing a hike or obtaining a particular rank. The boys get to set goals and are given opportunities to meet those goals. They are challenged. They get to climb real mountains and get to speak in front of a group. They are given responsibilities and are held accountable for their actions.

Very Proud

My son Ryan has gotten to experience a very full Scouting career. He started in the Cub Scouts and went on to eventually become an Eagle Scout. He stayed involved with the troop as a boy until the age of eighteen, and then he became an Assistant Scoutmaster. He is very proud of his accomplishments. I am as well. He says that the skills and values he learned as a scout have left a mark on him and that he uses them in the decisions he makes every day. I would have to say that I feel the same way about my own involvement in the Scouting program.

Chapter 6

Paper, Paper Everywhere

"Balancin' checkbooks, juggling bills
Thought there was nothing to it
Baby, now I know how you feel
What I don't know is how you do it"

- Lonestar "Mr. Mom[2]"

A Real Shock
When I first took a leave of absence from my job, I decided that I wanted to take on a lot of the paperwork responsibilities. I thought to myself, "How hard can this be?" I was in for the shock of my life ...

Everyone wants your attention. Of course, the best way to get that attention is to get some "face" time. The best kind of face time in my opinion involves meeting someone face-to-face in order to present your ideas or ask questions. This scenario is impractical in most cases since time is so limited. Therefore, most people try to contact you through the world of paper... and lots of it. The sources seem to be endless.

Mail Deliveries
First, there is the mail (including parcel deliveries). I'm referring to paperwork regarding our bills, charities, car registration, driver's license renewals, and of course, the infamous junk mail. I don't know how many times I do *not* have to place an order with catalog companies before they take a hint that I will not be placing an order anytime soon. This doesn't include a host of charities that just do not understand the statement, "We are committed to giving to you, but only once a year." I have actually called many of

---

[2] Writer: RON HARBIN, RICHARD VANCE MCDONALD, RICHIE MCDONALD, DON PFRIMMER
Lyrics © OLE MEDIA MANAGEMENT LP, Sony/ATV Music Publishing LLC

them and told them this over the phone, but they continue to seek additional funds several times a year. I am not sure that they realize that the money we give them doesn't make up for the cost of all the mail they send to us soliciting for another donation. I guess they are counting on us forgetting that we have only so much money to spend each year and that, just maybe, we will mail in another donation.

E-mail

Second, there is e-mail. This is sometimes redundant with the 'snail' mail, but either way, it is time-consuming. There are the e-mails from the various clubs we have joined over the years telling us of their weekly specials--(When will I learn not to fill in the e-mail address on the forms I fill out)?!?! I always enjoy the details from our friends and family on what is going on in their lives, but I know so much more today than I ever did in the past, that it is sometimes a bit overwhelming!

E-mail is a great tool. I have seen it used by the scouts reminding us of upcoming occasions and providing the forms we need to fill out to go on camping trips or other events. Politicians provide us with information on what is going on and give us the opportunity (i.e., more paperwork) to let them know how we feel regarding certain issues. Schools keep us up-to-date on what is going on in our kids' scholastic lives as well as provide us with details on deadlines and how to be better parents. I am beginning to believe that I can be a better parent if I were to spend more time with my kids rather than responding to the endless e-mails. E-mail is a great tool to learn of job opportunities and professional organization information. Eighty percent of what I receive via e-mail is useful, but there is just so much of it!

Third, there are the circulars and invoices left in our newspaper slot or on the front door of our house. There are many contractors that tell us of their leaf removal capabilities or how they are the best painter in town. I used to keep all of this information, however, it has gotten to be too much and now I just throw them away.

Did I Mention the Paperwork from School?

Next, there is the paperwork that comes home with the kids from school. Holy cow! Danielle's school used to send paperwork home with her every day. The parents revolted and the school decided to make Wednesday "paperwork" day. Ok, great. Now instead of cutting back on all of the paperwork I would get bombarded all on one day! Danielle would come home with a notebook filled with about fifteen pieces of paper that needed to be read and processed in one way or another. There were the field trip permission slips, the fundraising efforts, the book fairs, the personal information files, report cards, announcements, requests for volunteers, and the list goes on. I would write three or four checks every week to cover a wide range of "necessities" for the school. Then, of course, there were the doctor's forms. The kids need physical exams just to be in various school activities. The forms cover a myriad of topics from their vision to whether or not they have had Typhoid Fever. The forms are typically four to six pages long. The doctor would be responsible for filling out portions of the forms, but the parents (i.e., me) would need to fill out the balance. Trust me when I say that our children's medical history is well documented!

Training & More Training

Finally, there is the paperwork associated with our church and other social organizations that we are involved with. My goodness! This paperwork typically comes home with the kids when they return from a religious education class or scout meeting. There are the typical announcements, permission slips, and requests for money or supplies.

One aspect of these organizations that can drive me crazy is the adult training. When the schools, church, and Boy Scouts all ask you to take an Adult Protection Course before interacting with any children, it can get rather frustrating. To spend several hours a year learning all of the horrible things that we are not supposed to do to children is disheartening and discouraging. I sometimes wonder why more steps are not taken to really punish those who are actually committing these horrible acts against the children.

In the Boy Scout program, I have completed training programs for Youth Protection, Scoutmaster, New Leader Essentials, Weather Hazards, and Basic Training. I have also attended classes for Climb-on-Safely, Safe Swim Defense, Safety Afloat, Trek Safely, and Emergency First Response. I am also CPR-certified. I guess you could say I am highly trained.

I suppose that all of this training and paperwork are needed to successfully run our lives. I would love to hear what the trees have to say about all of this...but then again, that would probably require a lot of paperwork ...

Chapter 7

What's Cooking?

Learning How to Cook

When I was in Boy Scouts as a teenager, I first learned how to cook. It actually involved a good amount of work. There were no ovens or even propane stoves. We learned how to cook over an open fire using a fold-out cooking grate. There were many challenges to overcome. First you had to be able to build a fire. This can be daunting in and of itself ... just ask the man from Jack London's short story To Build a Fire. Second, you had to know how to cook the food. Third, you had to be able to cook several things at the same time. Finally, you had to be able to assess how the food was cooking since you had no idea what the temperature of the fire was. A meal of hamburgers and instant mashed potatoes was pretty common in those Scouting years. Looking back, it truly was an adventure. It cultivated in me a pretty good idea of how to cook when I went off on my own.

Different Approaches

After college, I lived on my own for three months before Michele and I got married. As a result, I got established in the kitchen that would soon be ours as a married couple. Now you need to understand that my personality type is one where I enjoy following directions. Some may say that I need directions. So when it comes to cooking, I am lost unless there is a recipe. I need the recipe and I follow every direction to the letter.

I was soon to find out that Michele's approach was very different. Michele is a very good cook who does not need any recipe. She is able to walk into a kitchen and just conjure something up. She makes wonderful stir-fry meals and incredible chicken dishes. When asked to repeat a recipe, she really can't duplicate it. It's just not the way she's wired.

Once we were married, we obviously had two conflicting approaches in the kitchen. I remember one morning we wanted to make pancakes. I told her that we couldn't since we did not have any pancake mix. Michele looked at me in a puzzled way and assured me we could. I then stuck to my guns and said we could not since there was no pancake mix. It was then that she enlightened me. She told me we could make them from scratch. She proceeded to show me how to make pancakes from flour, sugar, baking powder, milk, eggs, and cooking oil. It was like magic. It was then that I realized she had a gift that I did not have. I could cook but I could not 'wing it.'

A Fateful Night

We decided to take turns cooking until one fateful night. It was my turn to cook. I cannot remember what it was I was cooking, but I do recall that Michele was looking over my shoulder and giving me constructive criticism as to how I should be doing it. It was okay for the first ten minutes or so, but after a while, it got on my nerves and things started to break down. I asked her to leave reassuring her that I knew what I was doing. Occasionally I would ask for her suggestion, which was apparently an invitation to critique my technique. After a while, I began to think that I did not have to put up with this and decided that I didn't want to cook any more. Without me knowing it at the time, a decision in our life together was made at that moment. Michele was to do the primary cooking from that point on.

Fast Forward Nineteen Years

I had just stepped out of my job and became a stay-at-home dad. Out of necessity and convenience, it was decided that I would do the cooking. I was a bit rusty since I had only been doing limited cooking duty for the past two decades. I was good at grilling, and lunches were no problem. I could make a great breakfast with either pancakes, waffles, or my famous "killer eggs." Where I was woefully short on skills was in preparing dinner. I formulated a menu to choose from, but I have to admit that it was rather limited. There were hamburgers, hot dogs, grilled cheese, soup, spaghetti, pork loins, steak, macaroni and cheese and tacos.

Now before you become judgmental, I have to tell you that I always had vegetables. Sometimes I would serve a salad and other times it was frozen vegetables. What my menu lacked was variety. One of the staple food groups in my menu were the frozen foods. There was the frozen pizza, frozen stir fry meals, frozen crab cakes, and frozen tubs of pulled pork. Michele explained to me that if it wasn't fresh, that meant it was full of preservatives. I understood what she was saying; however the way I looked at it, there was a meal on the table.

One of the things I really struggled with was our busy lifestyle and how to accommodate preparing the dinnertime meal into our hectic day. I was always looking for the quick meals. That usually dictated my menu repertoire. It may not have been the healthiest menu, but it got the job done.

<u>Inspired to Try Something Different</u>

There were times when the complaining about the lack of variety or the healthiness of the menu got to me. I would decide to make a "real" meal. I remember the one time when I got inspired to try something different. At an awards ceremony, one of my neighbors made this incredible dish. She called it baked beans but, in my mind, it was a meal. There were the baked beans, but they were packed with bacon and ground beef as well. It was delicious, so I asked her for the recipe and decided to cook it myself. I reviewed the recipe and thought it would take about two hours to prepare and cook.

First I went to the grocery store and bought all of ingredients that we didn't already have. Then I started to prepare the dish which took about an hour. Then I put it in the oven for the allotted hour and ten minutes. I was very proud of my accomplishment, so when I placed it on the table, I was expecting some positive feedback. Well, the first comment was asking where the rest of the meal was. I explained that it was a meal in itself; that didn't seem to go over well. Everyone dug in and I was very disappointed to hear them say that it was okay but not great. I felt like I had been shot. Worse still, I resolved that it was back to the frozen foods.

A Few More Blunders along the Way

I have made many blunders as the primary cook in our house. There was the time where I was cooking a bag of ravioli. Now, in my defense, I clearly remember sometime in the past there was a food product where you threw the bag directly into the boiling water and the contents cooked inside the bag. At that point, you would remove the bag, cut it open, pour it into a dish, and eat. Well, that was not the case in this instance with the ravioli. And so when I threw this bag of ravioli into the pot of boiling water, I was surprised to see the water turn blue as all of the writing on the bag was boiled off and the bag began to melt. It was a disaster, and we did not have ravioli that night.

Then there was the time when I forget to de-shell the shrimp before cooking them. It was going to be a lovely pasta and shrimp dish. Everything was going well until we all took a bite of our first shrimp and discovered that it was very crunchy. I apologized as we all proceeded to take the shells off the remaining shrimp on our plates.

Another debacle was when I did not read the recipe correctly, so instead of putting one teaspoon of crushed red pepper into the dish, I put one tablespoon. The meal looked great, but none of us were prepared for the spicy sensation that awaited us. We were all laughing as our mouths erupted with the tanginess of the overly spiced food. I clearly remember Danielle's lips turned blue. We all got a huge laugh over this particular blunder!

A funny transition occurred after the first year I became a stay-at-home dad. I am not sure how it happened. It just did, and I guess I let it happen subconsciously. Michele became the primary dinnertime cook once again. Thank goodness! I guess she got tired of the "Dad menu" and wanted us to eat a little healthier. My tummy thanked her for it.

Chapter 8

Good News?

<u>A Turning Point in my Viewing Habits</u>

For me it started in the mid 1980's. Michele and I had just gotten married. We were living blissfully in New London, Connecticut. We were just starting our life as a married couple and didn't have a care in the world. We spent our weekends and holidays going to the local park, taking in a movie, having a beer or two, and watching television. I will never forget the news story that changed my television viewing habits forever. The story came on about a house that had exploded. It seemed that there had been a gas leak and when the husband went down into the basement to try and remedy the problem, the house blew up. Tragically, he died. Now, I can only think of one or two things worse than losing your spouse, so you would think that a certain amount of respect and dignity would be used in a news story such as this one...Well, this is where I got an education to prove that I was dead wrong (no pun intended). Picture this ... There was the news reporter live on the site of the tragedy. He was standing in front of what was once the house of this retired elderly couple. Instead of a house there was now a crater and lots of debris. Standing beside him was the widow whom had graciously offered to be interviewed. I stood there in absolute horror when he asked her how she felt when they were pulling her husband's dead body out of the rubble. How could someone ask such a thoughtless and rude question? I was simply flabbergasted and decided that I would no longer be a regular watcher of the news.

Am I against television? No, I am not. In fact, I am for it. It can have a huge positive impact on us as a society. It can entertain us through tasteful sitcoms and comedy acts. It can instill us with passion through a good movie or a beautiful song. It can inspire us with kind acts others bestow upon their fellow man. It can create pride in us as we root for our favorite team. It can educate us on our history, our current technology, and our government. The list goes on and on. What is truly sad is that a majority of the media does not look for the good in our society but instead looks for the bad.

<u>A Very Memorable 90 Seconds</u>

I will never forget when I was visiting my parents and the local news had just started. I decided that I would count the number of horrific news stories that would be presented. The first story was about a robbery that had gone wrong and ended in murder. The second and third stories were about fires, one that resulted in the injury to a local firefighter. The fourth story was regarding a traffic accident that had put two people into shock trauma and the prognosis did not look good. The fifth story was about a young girl who was missing and there were no new leads as to her whereabouts. Foul play was suspected. This story really upset me since I have a young daughter myself. I could no longer watch the news with my parents. I looked at my watch. A minute and a half had passed since the newscast had begun.

Does the news create anxiety? Most definitely! How can anyone forget what happened after the anthrax scare which occurred right after 9-11? I remember all of the people who fled to Mexico to get Cipro which is an antidote to anthrax that was unavailable in the United States. Was this crazed action necessary? I don't believe so. Then there was the time when Ryan and I were watching TV together. We had just flown to Atlanta for a competition that Ryan was in. He was about fourteen. Anyway, there we sat in the train taking us from the airport to downtown Atlanta. There was a huge TV in each car that was showing the latest news. There were your typical murders, fires, rapes, and scandals. Just when it struck me how silly it was to force us to watch these horrible stories, Ryan leaned over to me and without any prompting by me said, "I don't feel safe here." I could not blame him. According to the news the entire city was on fire and under siege. We were anxious and did not get the chance to develop our own impression. The news had already done that for us.

Loop of Terror

Then there is the format that I like to call the "loop of terror." It is found on the cable stations that run only news. I frequently find myself at car dealerships waiting for several hours while my car is being serviced. The dealerships are kind enough to provide a TV for our entertainment while we wait. However, I cringe when the stations are set to one of these all-news channels. Being a captive audience, I came to several realizations. First, these channels repeat the same stories every thirty minutes or so (hence the name I have given to this dreaded "loop"). Second, all of the stories are about as sensational as they can be and made even more sensational by how they are presented. To present the stories, the newscasters use words that create anxiety. Words and phrases like 'complete devastation', 'burned and charred', 'utter', 'horrific', 'raging', 'deadly rampage', 'raw sewage', 'massive wildfire' and my personal favorite: 'disaster of unimaginable proportions.' Finally, these channels primarily focus on these anxiety-provoking stories.

The Good News is Definitely There

It is my opinion that the media needs to take responsibility. What I mean by responsibility is that they need to take a look at the forest and stop focusing on the individual trees. They need to look at what impact they are having on us as a society in the long term instead of getting ratings that night. There is a lot of good in the world. It is my opinion that 90 percent of what is 'newsworthy' is good news. Why don't they report on that?

I will give you my theory and you can take it or leave it. As human beings, we are drawn to the sensational. For example, I believe that most people slow down at the car wreck on the highway so they might catch the glimpse of person crushed under a car or someone who has been decapitated. We do the same thing with what's on TV. Whoever is showing the most sensational story that night is the story we are going to watch. For me, the best stories are the ones that inspire. I want to learn about the volunteer efforts being done by the Boy Scouts and not how some scouts were killed by a tornado. I want to learn about the way the Catholic Church is making a positive difference in the lives of millions of people throughout the world with their humanitarian aid instead of how some priests conducted heinous acts.

The media seems to have no boundaries when it comes to how far they will go. Take the story of Mother Teresa who is probably one of the greatest people to live in the past one hundred years. When she died we learned about her life of total commitment to the least fortunate. The thing that kills me is that the media couldn't help themselves to move past the story and talk about her "dark times." In fact, they did not even take the time to get the story right. They just assumed that she had lost her faith and that is the way they left it. Why couldn't they have gotten their facts straight before presenting such a damning story?

What is really sad is that I believe the news doesn't even realize the amount of power they have over us. They have a huge role in forming our opinions of other countries, of other people, of how we should do things, of why we should do things. They don't understand this incredible power and they sometimes go about their jobs very irresponsibly. I will give you another example. Do you remember the Presidential Election of 2000 where the news media stated that Florida was going to go to the Democratic candidate Al Gore? Then they flipped and stated that it was going to George Bush, and then they changed it to "too close to call." Meanwhile, the rest of the country was still voting. Some people were watching the results as they came in and were wondering what to do. And I think some people on the West coast weren't going to go out to vote if they thought a landslide was occurring on the East coast. The media shouldn't be making the call. Let the voters make the call. Taking this concept one step further, I believe there should be a media blackout until every person has the chance to vote. Once all the votes are in, then they should present the results. Keep the media out of it since they can influence our mindset.

Look for the good news. It is there.

Chapter 9

Lending a Hand

"Idle hands and idle minds are surely the sign of the devil."

- Author Unknown

Taking a "Thousand Points of Light" to Heart

Unbeknownst to President George H. W. Bush, he had a large impact on my life. In his 2002 State of the Union Address, he put out a very interesting challenge to all of the citizens of the United States with his "Thousand Points of Light." He asked that everyone volunteer for a total of two years. He said that the world would be a much better place if we were to donate our time. I would have to agree with that and really took this philosophy to heart. I have always been a volunteer, but I stepped up my efforts when I first became a stay-at-home dad. I considered my change in employment status as an opportunity to volunteer and make a positive difference in my community. There are many worthy organizations and I found myself quickly immersed in many of them.

As you have probably already surmised, Boy Scouts has been an integral part of my life for quite some time now. I participated for about ten years as a boy and find myself participating again as an adult. For many years I have been an Adult Leader in a variety of capacities including Den Leader, Committee Member, and Assistant Scoutmaster. The joke in Boy Scouts is that it is only "one hour a week." Well, I can tell you that it is more like twenty hours a week, between the meetings, camping trips, summer camp, courts of honor, service projects, working with the older scouts, merit badge counseling, e-mails, phone calls, planning and … You get the idea. It is a great organization, but it takes a lot of effort to get it to work right.

Marriage Encounter has been a part of Michele's and my life since 1989. Marriage Encounter, for those of you who may not have heard of it before, is a weekend couples' enrichment program designed to make good marriages great. It is kind of like giving your marriage a tune-up. Michele and I were so touched by our original weekend that we have continued our journey. Things we have done include being a presenting couple on the weekends, giving pulpit talks at churches throughout our community, helping to plan and carry out a national convention in our area, putting together displays for our church's Ministry Fair, attending meetings, and doing hundreds of talks. This organization has helped to make us the strong couple we are today and we enjoy giving back to it as a result. Another benefit is that Marriage Encounter has allowed us to volunteer our time while being together.

Drawing Inspiration and Fulfillment

Our church is a huge source of inspiration to us. When the four of us attend church together, I feel like all of our spiritual gas tanks are being filled. It gives us a chance to be with others who have similar values, hear the readings from the Bible, and take in the sermon together. The sense of community in our church is amazing and is one of the factors that led to my conversion to Catholicism many years ago. It then came naturally to us to become more involved in our church.

Together we are a greeter family. Additionally, our two kids have been involved with the religious education program and have served as an altar server, audio specialist, banner bearer, confirmation teacher, and choir member. Our kids have also served the homeless at a local kitchen. Danielle has been in numerous plays sponsored by the church. Michele is a Eucharistic Minister and I have served as an usher and Director of Religious Education. As a member of the Pastoral Council for four years, I served as Vice Chair for one year and the Chair for another year. Later on I became involved with the Knights of Columbus. Michele and I have served as confirmation teachers for the 10th grade class. Our involvement keeps us grounded as individuals, as a couple, and as a family.

Involvement in our Kids' Lives

We stay involved with our kids' school lives. Besides attending award ceremonies, PTA meetings, orientations, college preparatory seminars, American Education Week, and parent-teacher conferences, I have also volunteered in many ways. I have chaperoned numerous field trips including trips to Washington, DC and the National Aquarium, as well as local trips to a corn maze, amusement park, singing competitions, band competitions, fundraising events, and a mini-city experience staffed by the students. The list goes on and on.

I'm a lucky man to have such great kids

I have also presented at the kids' schools during "Career Day." I began doing this when the kids were in pre-school and continued the tradition all the way through high school. (I chose to present the career of Civil Engineer and not being a stay-at-home dad. If I had presented about being a stay-at-home dad, I could have joked with them about having to volunteer for a lot of things including making presentations at Career Day). When the kids were in middle school, I assisted in running the canoe station at the school's all-day event called "Bay Days." It was a lot of fun, but I don't recommend throwing a lot of novices into lots of canoes all at the same time!

I have also been a library volunteer, lunch volunteer, science class lab assistant, and field day assistant. I am sure my kids dreaded me being there, but I wanted to show each of them that they were important in my eyes and that I was literally 'putting my money where my mouth was' by being involved in their school activities right alongside them.

Down-time with the kids is always great

Extracurricular Involvement

This then brings me to the kids' extracurricular activities. There have been many over the years in which I've been involved in one way or the other. I always assisted in coaching Ryan's baseball, soccer, and basketball teams. I was also co-coach of his robotics team that won the state championship and then advanced onto the World Championship held in Atlanta, Georgia. I chaperoned jazz band trips and helped him prepare for his three 'People to People' trips. (People to People is an excellent organization in which students travel abroad and are ambassadors for the United States).

With Danielle, I kept busy working on the sets for her plays, and planning and teaching skills at some of her Girl Scout meetings. It seemed like I was always taking the kids to and from their dance practices, piano lessons, gymnastic classes, choir rehearsals, youth group meetings, lacrosse practices, yearbook meetings, and service projects. When I look at my kids' lives, I realize that the saying "The nut doesn't fall far from the tree" is probably true.

Another yearly activity I have volunteered for is the 'Relay for Life' event. This event is sponsored by the American Cancer Society. Not only does the event raise funds for the research and educational needs of cancer, but it also honors those who are battling the disease and pays tribute to those who lost the battle. I have been doing this for about twelve years, and it means as much to me today as it did when I first started. It seems that no one is immune from the effects of cancer. My grandmother died of ovarian cancer when I was a teenager. My cousin Steve died at the age of forty-four from brain cancer, and Michele's dad died of Mesothelioma a few years ago. I am hopeful that there will be a cure for this dreadful disease soon and I would like to think that I am making a difference.

So Many Positive Impacts

I guess that helping my family, friends and neighbors is a form of volunteering. I know that I help them out a lot more now than I did when I was working full-time. When I reflect on some of the things I have done to help others, I have to smile. I have:

- ✓ Taught neighborhood kids how to parallel park their cars preparing for their driving tests
- ✓ Removed pieces of a chimney from a roof that was hit by lightning
- ✓ Replaced light bulbs in hard-to-reach places
- ✓ Changed smoke detector alarm batteries

- ✓ Helped neighbors find contractors for building sidewalks, sealing driveways, replacing driveways, and providing various tree services
- ✓ Plowed driveways
- ✓ Changed car tires (almost died on this one)
- ✓ Jump-started cars with dead batteries
- ✓ Filled car tires with air
- ✓ Responded to numerous home alarms (I learned that the police sometimes get itchy when you show up offering assistance)
- ✓ Rearranged a lot of the furniture in a house. (I wish I could have been there when the husband came home after the house had been rearranged)!
- ✓ Checked up on heat pumps
- ✓ Played Santa Claus at a holiday party
- ✓ Reattached a front bumper on a car that got into an altercation with a basketball pole (I promised not tell anyone who this was)!
- ✓ Provided keys to get into houses (their own houses, of course)
- ✓ Installed lawnmower blades
- ✓ Cut lawns
- ✓ Removed unwanted brush and vegetation from steep hillsides (very steep)
- ✓ Checked on houses after severe weather
- ✓ Picked up tree debris after significant storms
- ✓ Helped someone sell their business (This was an effort taking several hundred hours of my time)
- ✓ Unclogged toilets
- ✓ Unclogged gutters
- ✓ Figured out the gas supply on a hot water heater

- ✓ Reviewed contracts
- ✓ Attended public meetings to speak up for our community
- ✓ Helped dispose of worn American flags properly
- ✓ Painted interior rooms
- ✓ Fixed dishwashers
- ✓ Helped pack for moving
- ✓ Reviewed and edited books being written by others
- ✓ Helped close down vacation homes for the off season
- ✓ Organized community yard sales
- ✓ Recapped pickup trucks
- ✓ Booked cruises on behalf of others
- ✓ Determined fair rental values for vacation properties
- ✓ Wrote letters on behalf of others
- ✓ Set mousetraps
- ✓ Took care of dogs and birds
- ✓ Lobbied to have our community roads repaired
- ✓ Performed troubleshooting of plumbing problems
- ✓ Visited people in the hospital
- ✓ Taught teenagers how to maintain their cars
- ✓ Helped kids start their own businesses
- ✓ Researched Bed & Breakfasts on behalf of others
- ✓ Bought Christmas gifts on someone else's behalf
- ✓ Picked up and dropped off kids to various meetings, trips, and events

I feel fortunate to have had the opportunity as a stay-at-home-dad to help others.

Lots of Funny Moments Along the Way

There have been some very funny stories associated with the various volunteering I did over the years. Here are just a few:

Story #1 – It's a Bloody Mess – Whenever you volunteer, you need to be trained. However, what it is you are trained for can be a surprise. Ryan had moved on from elementary school to middle school. Many of the parents wanted to continue to volunteer at the same level of intensity that they did in elementary school. Well, it seems that the middle school was not really expecting this much enthusiasm, but when they learned that the parents wanted to help out, the school decided to invite the parents to a meeting. As you now know, I am all about volunteering and so I went to this meeting.

At the meeting, I was expecting to learn how to use the copier, where the supplies were located, how to gain access into the school, and other things that would allow us to help the teachers. I think that these topics had been briefly discussed at some point during the twenty minute meeting, but then again, maybe they weren't. All I remember for sure was the presentation by the school nurse which seemed to last forever. She wanted to be crystal clear as to what we were to do in the event of an injury involving blood. She went on and on about the dangers of having direct contact with blood since it is the carrier of all kinds of diseases. She told us about the gloves that were to be used, how to clean up blood, and how she was to be contacted immediately in any event involving blood. She did not discuss any other types of injuries, just those involving blood. My impression was that there was going to be a lot of blood during any volunteering efforts at the middle school.

Story #2 - Congratulations on Your Stick Handling! - Sometimes it is not the volunteering that is perplexing, but the participating. Ryan was about six or seven years old when he decided that he wanted to give lacrosse a try. Michele and I were open to him trying new things so we could weed out the ones that he did not enjoy. We had a feeling that he would not succeed in lacrosse since he did not have the "eye of the tiger" when it came to sports. Let's just say that Michele and I witnessed numerous occasions that, when it came to sports, Ryan preferred talking to everyone on the field rather than actually playing the game.

In the case of clinic lacrosse, we had nothing to worry about since there would be no games. In fact, after a couple of months of "practices" Ryan knew how to hold the stick, pick the ball up off the ground, and walk around with the ball in the wicket. The kids may have even tried to throw the ball to each other. The trophies were not at the last practice so we had to pick them up from the coach after the season ended. First off, I was a bit surprised that there was any trophy. I mean, the boys didn't even play a game! I decided to go anyway. Ryan and I got to the parking lot and there was the coach leaning up against the back of his pickup truck. We parked the car, got out, and walked over to the coach. I expected him to produce the typical ten to twelve-inch-high trophy. Well, he reached into the bed of his truck and produced this mammoth two-foot-high trophy! I thought there must have been some huge mistake since it appeared that Ryan had won the NCAA Lacrosse tournament. That trophy is still one of the largest trophies that Ryan has ever received, and it was all because he learned how to hold a stick.

Now it causes me a lot of heartburn regarding these stupid trophies to begin with. The philosophy is this: Everyone gets the same trophy no matter how well your team does.

That is simply ridiculous! That is not how real life works. When you do well in real life, you get rewarded. When you do poorly, you suffer the consequences. It is my opinion that you can have trophies, but they should be for the first, second, and third place teams. The other teams can get a certificate or medal of participation, but not a trophy.

Story #3 – It's Gonna Be Cold – Danielle participated in the Girl Scout cookie sales every year and did very well. Besides door-to-door sales, her troop would typically hold sales at the local grocery store inside the lobby as shoppers would come and go. This one particular year they also decided to sell the cookies at an outdoor mall around the end of October. Now Maryland is not Minnesota as far as coldness goes, but it can get a bit nippy. In addition, all of my outdoor training taught me that once you get cold, it is hard to heat back up, especially when you are sitting around selling Girl Scout cookies! To top it all off, the weatherman was calling for rain that evening and the temperature was in the high thirties.

I kept telling the girls to dress in layers and to make sure they had rain gear. Ponchos would be okay, but a rain jacket with rain pants would be preferred. I tried to impress upon them that once they got wet, they would not be able to get dry again until they went inside and were able to change their clothes. I explained to them that it was a potential recipe for disaster unless they planned appropriately. We arrived at the mall to sell cookies. Danielle and I looked like we were dressed for a trip to the North Pole, but were determined to stay dry and warm. The mother who was running the event had on a very stylish fall jacket including fur on the trim. She looked very nice, but I had serious doubts that she was going to make it through the four-hour shift we had planned. She was full of energy and assured me that she would be all right. She had an umbrella! We went our separate ways since there were two stations. She was in charge of one station while I was in charge of the other. Cookie sales were kind of slow but we were getting promises of people coming back to buy more. I was beginning to believe that this was going to be fun. Not twenty minutes went by when the mom in charge drove over to our station to say that she couldn't take it anymore and she was going home. I did not want to say "I told you so," but I did tell her so ...

Story #4 – I Checked "Assistant Coach" – I was home one night when I got a phone call asking me where I was. The answer seemed obvious to me since they called me at home. However, I played along and asked what was happening. They informed me that there was a soccer coach meeting at that moment and that my presence was required. I was shocked since I knew that I was not a soccer coach. There was no way for me to be a soccer coach since I had so many night and weekend commitments that would not allow me to attend all of the practices and games. How could this scenario have developed? Apparently I had checked off the "Assistant Coach" box in the parent involvement section when filling out Ryan's registration form. I figured that I ended up being an assistant coach on every sports team my kids get involved with so I may as well check off the box. Obviously, from the league organizer's perspective, this meant that I was willing to be a coach. So, I learned a valuable lesson that day. If you want to be an assistant coach, do not check any boxes. If you want to be coach, then check off the assistant coach box. "So what happened?" you may ask. I did go on to co-coach with another parent. Unfortunately, we did not have a strong grasp on what it took to be a successful soccer team coach and we went on to lose a lot of games. We did have fun along the way.

Story #5 – It is so Life-like – Danielle has been in the Girl Scouts since she was in kindergarten. I have tried to help her out in a number of ways by making sure all of her patches got sewn on, filling out all of the numerous forms, working with her on various badges, and helping her sell cookies. One of my favorite tasks was leading several of her meetings and teaching the girls some new skills. I figured that it was good that they have some positive male influences in their lives and I tried to teach them skills that maybe some of the other parents didn't know.

The one class that got me particularly excited was the one on auto care. I am pretty meticulous when it comes to being prepared, so one of the requirements was to change a tire. I had never changed the tire on our minivan so I decided to try it prior to the Girl Scout meeting. Everything was going well on my test run until I went to lower the spare tire from the underside of the van. The lowering device jammed and then broke. This meant that I had to go to my service center and get it fixed. I had to chuckle insanely when I paid the $200 bill. Here it was that I was trying to do something good for my community and I had to pay a $200 bill. Oh well, I assumed that things couldn't get worse so I plowed on.

The day of the meeting finally came. They were calling for intermittent thunderstorms that day so I kept my eye on the weather. Some of the instruction I could do indoors but some of it, including the changing of the tire, had to be done outdoors. When I first arrived, it was raining moderately and the weatherman was predicting that the storms would taper off, so I decided to do the indoor portion first. Everything was going very smoothly until I ran out of indoor activities and had to go outdoors to change the tire. Well that is when the skies opened up and it was a genuine deluge. Fortunately, the way I staged the minivan allowed the girls to safely watch me change the tire from under the cover of the building. I, on the other hand, was not so lucky. So there I was soaking wet, shouting over the roar of the pounding rain, saying, "These conditions may be like the ones you will encounter in a real scenario when you are changing a tire."

Story #6 - Desperate Housewives - Danielle was enrolled in a private school for several years. It was a very positive and wonderful experience for her. One of the great things was that the parents had to be involved in order to make the school a success. This helped create a community environment amongst all of the families with children enrolled in the school. I mentioned previously the many things we did as a family to help the school out. One of my funniest memories is when Danielle's fifth grade teacher asked me to volunteer for a particular event.

Danielle's teacher was a good friend, so I trusted her when she asked me to assist her. I wanted to help out (of course), so I said yes. As the event drew nearer, I started to get details on what I was expected to do. At first I thought I misunderstood what I was doing, but it turned out I was right on the money. Apparently, I was going to be dressed up by the kids as one of the crazy wives from the TV show "Desperate Housewives." And so I got into a dress, put on a wig, got the full make-up treatment and was accessorized. I got to strut my stuff much to the entertainment of the kids and all of the other adults in attendance. It was an interesting and unique experience for me. I guess I got a taste of what it was like to be Bugs Bunny, one of the biggest cross-dressers of all time!

As you can see, I found many ways to get plugged into the community and essentially became a "professional volunteer." The high water mark for me as a volunteer was shortly after I dropped out of the workforce. The stars seemed to collide as I found myself preparing for and participating in a national convention for Marriage Encounter, preparing for and attending summer camp with my son's Boy Scout troop, helping with the sets and serving as back stage crew associated with my daughter's play, being involved with my church's Pastoral Council, and finally, volunteering at the local library. In one month's time I volunteered close to 300 hundred hours. Keep in mind that the average person works about 173 hours a month. It was a pretty exhausting time and I remember thinking, "What have I gotten myself into?"

Now this particular experience was the exception and not the rule as I typically volunteered approximately 140 to 150 hours a month. Did I enjoy what I was doing? Yes. Was I making my community stronger by getting involved just as President Bush had predicted? Yes. Was it insane? Yes. When you consider that Alex Rodriguez, the third baseman for the New York Yankees, makes $33 million per year for playing a game and I got $0 per year for trying to improve the world we live in, I would have to say that it is insane! Now, would I trade my life for that of Alex Rodriguez? Most definitely not!

Chapter 10

Bingo!!

New Discoveries

When I first started my journey as Mr. Mom, I was not exactly sure what to expect. I sat down and established a routine to get the chores done around the house, meet our social obligations, run errands, and just keep our lives moving forward in a productive fashion. However, this experience truly was unchartered territory since I had held a job since I was fifteen years old and really did not know any other kind of lifestyle other than to get up every day and go to work. I was not sure what would happen, but I was determined to go into it with an open mind. What happened was truly wonderful as I was given the opportunity to cultivate the relationships in my life.

The first thing I noticed was my time spent with the kids. It felt like a true blessing to be this intimately involved with their lives. I was able to witness their daily routines much more closely than I ever had in the past. Whether I was chaperoning on one of Danielle's field trips, taking the kids to a doctor's appointment, being director of their religious education program, or driving Ryan to a Boy Scout function, I was a part of their daily lives. I also enjoyed watching them interact with their friends, which helped me get to know their friends as well.

It wasn't only my kids that I got to know better; it was my family as well. My brother and I did a couple of weekend camping trips together. We would set up a tent at a park, cook greasy food on the propane stove, and talk about what was going on in our lives. It was fun just hanging out together and being brothers. I would also spend a couple of weeks every year with my parents. I would help them with various handyman projects around their house. More importantly, my time interacting with them was an opportunity to just be a part of their everyday lives and to let them know how important they were to me.

Finding my Calling

I remember after being at home for about a year that I asked Michele and the kids to assess how things were going. I wanted to find out what was working and what I needed to improve upon. The feedback was very constructive and I took it to heart. The comment that struck me the most was from Danielle. She was about eight years old at the time and she said that it had been a highlight to have me around so we could hang out and do things together. Other people in my life said I appeared to be happier – and I was. I felt that I was doing something constructive with my life including making a positive difference in hundreds of people's lives. I truly felt that this was my calling and God's plan for me.

I actually saw myself slowing down to smell the roses. I was embracing the philosophy that life is a journey, not a destination. Up until the time I became a stay-at-home dad, it seemed that I was always striving to meet the next goal and I was racing to some finish line.

An example of my new-found attitude is in my interaction with my godchildren. I have seven in all: James, Samantha, Leia, Julian, John, Kiely and Mary. They are sons and daughters of family and friends, and they bring joy into my life as I have watched them grow up, experience life, and develop into fine young men and women. I believe it is one thing to hold the title of godparent and another one to try and act as one. The challenge is that there are only so many hours in the day. Additionally, the fact that they live throughout the U.S. as well as outside the country makes it even more tricky. However, by being a stay-at-home dad, I was able to interact with them on a more meaningful level. I thought to myself, "How can I be a good godparent and pass on to them good values as well as life lessons?" Then it dawned on me that I can write letters to my godchildren. It does not cost anything, except my time and some stamps, and it could be something they can keep and refer to for the rest of their lives. This idea has had an impact on my life as well as theirs. In fact, I got a comment from my high school friend Doug, whose daughter I am godfather for. He said that he appreciated the fact that I took the time to stay in touch and that I show I care about him and his family. His words touched me. I felt God's presence once again in my life through his words. I am truly blessed ...

Chapter 11

One Thing Leads to Another

Looking for a New Project or Two

I needed something to do. Sure, I was busy the first year or so doing all of the projects that had been put off for years. There was the construction of the patio, raking all of the debris from the entire lawn, the terracing of the back yard, painting the entire house, but I needed more…

I found myself at the local block party engaged in a conversation with one of our neighbors. They mentioned that they needed a retaining wall built in their front yard. Well, I had built around twenty retaining walls in our lawn due to its steep nature, so I told them I could build a wall for them. One thing led to another and I found myself working for them. I genuinely loved it. I was outside using my hands and I was my own boss. I could make my own schedule and still could make our family my number one priority.

Coming in from a long day of working outside --
My attire got a grin out of Danielle!

Challenges Early On

On the one hand, there were a lot of good things about this situation; however, there were also a lot of "challenges." The first thing I learned about was certification to become a contractor. A contractor has to go through training and then take a test. I am not sure if it was the original intention, but in my opinion the purpose of the state certification for all contractors should be to ensure that the public is getting a quality product. It turns out that that is not the case. It has nothing to do with your vocation but rather on how to run your business ethically. I had plenty of ethical training as a civil engineer, so I found this effort to be redundant and unnecessary. The whole process of the state certification costs about $1,600. Considering I made less than six times that much in the first year, I decided to bypass the certification.

Then there were the tools needed to get the job done right. I had some tools, but I needed more to be able to do this type of work on a large scale. The proper tools were needed for design, layout, and construction. Some I did purchase and others I had to live without. For instance, it would have been nice to have a pick-up truck instead of the minivan, but I did discover the minivan to be a very versatile vehicle. I often considered getting a plate compactor which would have allowed me to tamp down the gravel below most of the structures I built. However, it was hard to justify spending $3,000 on this tool. I did not even consider getting liability insurance or workman's compensation insurance. I had to walk away with something in my pocket!

Sitting down with our accountant at the end of the year was especially heartbreaking. After the first year I had made about $10,000 and had about $1,100 in overhead expenses which excluded time I spent pulling together proposals for jobs. Anyway, the accountant informed us that we had to pay approximately half of what I made to the local, state and federal governments. In addition, there was Social Security and Medicare which I was more than willing to pay. However, I did not like the fact that I had to pay Social Security taxes twice...once as the employee and once as the employer. When I asked if I would get twice the Social Security payments when I retire, I was told "no." I was cutting all of the corners as far as expenses were concerned, busting my you-know-what and clearing about $3,000 per year. My appreciation for what contractors do was increasing!

Some Rejections & Disappointments

Then there was the disappointment in not getting a job. I took great pains to get my numbers correct. I used various pieces of literature to develop a fair unit labor cost as well as the time it would take to build certain landscaping structures. I would go to all of the suppliers to figure out material costs including delivery. Some estimates took over twenty hours to compile, so when I would give a client my estimate and they would say "no," it was sometimes difficult to bear especially when it was the second or third rejection in a row. Sometimes a client had fallen upon hard times, but sometimes it was just that they didn't have a good idea what they were getting into.

I remember one client who wanted a set of stairs in their backyard. I did a preliminary layout so I could develop the cost estimate and found that they needed eleven steps. After putting together the cost estimate, I called and informed them that the cost was $2,500 including materials and labor. They were surprised at the cost so I asked them what they anticipated the cost to be. They said $400. When I informed them that the cost of the supplies alone was $1,800, they said they couldn't do it.

Another client called me to give them a quote to build two rather significant projects in their back yard. They were a younger couple and had already completed some beautiful projects in their back yard. Up to that point, the husband had been doing all of the work himself. However, they decided they needed some help finishing the back yard work. The first project was a large stone staircase down to a lower level in their yard complemented with large stones strewn around the staircase. The second project was a pathway with several small steps. I believed that they were biting off more than they could chew, so I convinced them to have me develop an estimate for just the large staircase project and then we would take it from there.

Once again, I spent approximately twenty hours developing an estimate. The project was complicated by the fact that I had to rent a rather significant piece of equipment to move the stones from the street down to the worksite. The piece of equipment had a forklift on the front and was about the size of a car. It cost about $1,000 to rent. Anyway, I finished the estimate and called them. I told the husband that the project was $7,000 including materials and labor. I asked him what he thought and he said he thought the cost was high. He informed me that he was in the process of getting estimates from other contractors. He said he would call me back with his final decision but I thought I would never hear from him again. I was pleasantly surprised when two weeks went by and he called me back. He said he got one other contractor (out of the many he contacted) to come out to look at the projects. The contractor proceeded to tell them all of the things they should do and then told them that it would cost $5,000-10,000 to develop a drawn up "plan" for his vision. The contractor did not even bother to give them a cost to do the two projects they had wanted. I then asked the owner what his plans were. He said he was going to try and do the work himself. I understand why the process developed the way it did, but in the end it was still difficult not to get the job.

The Return was Worth It

Overall, I really enjoyed running the business. It was never overwhelming, and I really enjoyed seeing what was accomplished once each job was completed. Another huge benefit is that I got to know my clients very well. Some have been family and some have been friends. Some are people I hardly knew but whom I now consider to be good friends.

Chapter 12

I Want That Job!

Could this be the Perfect Career?

Since I began a career where I was outside most of the time, the weather became a critical part of my job. If I was placing concrete or painting windows, I needed to know the temperature and whether or not it was going to rain. Sounds pretty easy especially in today's highly technological society where information is everywhere. I soon learned that this was not the case.

My primary source was the Weather Channel. They would show you the daily forecast plus the extended outlook. I soon learned that their predictions/educated guesses were not very accurate. They would be changing the forecast for any one given day all the way up until that day. Then they would call for "partly cloudy" and it would rain, or they would call for "rain" and it would be sunny. So then I thought I would get smart and start referring to other sources as well. I would go to the local news stations for information as well as the local paper. Once again they would give the daily as well as extended forecasts. What I was learning was that each source had a different prediction. Most would be wrong, but someone would typically be right. Unfortunately, I found that it was never the same source that was right. I was at a loss!

I did eventually have a revelation: the perfect job is to be a weatherman. It seems to me that it doesn't matter if you are wrong or right—you just need to make your daily predictions. Now I don't know the exact percentage of time that typical weather sources are accurate. To me it only seems like twenty percent of the time. However, even if the reverse is true and the weather sources are accurate eighty percent of the time, it would still leave a significant margin of error. This sounds like a dream come true, since I imagine that most employers would find this success rate unacceptable ... Where do I sign up?

Chapter 13

Errand Boy

Errands to be done today:

- ✓ Blood sample
- ✓ Go to the dump
- ✓ Get Christmas card picture with the kids
- ✓ Take in hot tub water sample
- ✓ Take in cat's stool sample
- ✓ Purchase liquor (lots of it)

Errands and More Errands

It takes a lot of effort to run a household effectively. I learned this firsthand when I first became a stay-at-home dad. The amount of errands that need to be run can become overwhelming. There is the trip to the post office, the re-stocking of hot tub chemicals, dry cleaning, prescriptions filled at the pharmacy, visits to the library, buying gifts for various occasions, purchasing the gallon of milk, filling the car with gas, getting office supplies, processing film, finding birthday and anniversary cards, dropping stuff off at our church, banking, acquiring yard supplies, household project supplies, haircuts, renting movies, visiting the liquor store, taking the vehicles in for service and maintenance, emissions inspections, grocery shopping, dropping off all sorts of equipment for repairs and maintenance, taking the cat to the vet, and trips to Goodwill and the dump, ... just to name a few!

Of course, there are also errands associated with the kids including taking them to doctor appointments, dentist appointments, orthodontist appointments, and eye doctor appointments. There are the dance practices and recitals, piano practice and recitals, Boy Scout meetings, Boy Scout outings, Girl Scout meetings, Girl Scout field trips, choir rehearsals, baseball games, soccer games, play practices, chorale rehearsals (yes, this is not choir), Christian Youth Group meetings, religious education classes, Tae Kwon Do classes, Robotics meetings, debate matches, community service projects, art shows, and the list goes on and on. I did not realize how much there was to do until I was doing it all myself.

My Philosophy

When it comes to running errands, my philosophy is not to go out every time an item is needed. In fact, I will collect errands and do them all at once. Even so, I typically do ten to fifteen errands at a time. They are done once a week and it takes me six to eight hours to complete them. (Incidentally, my record was twenty-three stops in one errands run). And of course, running an errand is not simply going out, buying something, and then returning home. Sometimes up-front prep work is needed and debriefing work is needed as well.

Grocery shopping is a perfect example. Before stepping out the door, I need to compile a list. I will go through items needed for breakfast, lunch, and dinner. Then I will look at our current stock of toiletry items, paper products, cleaning items, pet food, and anything else in order to determine what may be needed. Some of the prep work also includes reviewing the weekly circulars and clipping coupons for those items we typically purchase. So I probably spend half an hour a week clipping coupons, one hour preparing a list and compiling coupons, a couple of hours traveling and shopping, and then an hour putting away the groceries. It drives me a little nuts when it takes as long to put things away as it does to go out and purchase them.

Some Introspection

I am also taking better care of myself now that I have the time to. I go to the dentist twice a year, get a physical once a year, and I have started seeing a dermatologist. I have to do a sidebar here: Looking back at my career choice, I should have become a dermatologist. Let me explain.

The first time I went I had to undergo the typical first visit. Of course there was lots of paperwork since it was the first time I had visited this doctor. I spent around forty-five minutes in the waiting room filling out mundane paperwork and also … waiting. Then I was escorted back to the room where the doctor was to see me. There I waited for another forty-five minutes. When the doctor came into the room, it was a whirlwind. He quickly looked over my face (I guess he deemed that the rest of my body was not worthy looking over), and he asked if I used sunscreen. He then turned around, walked across the room, and proceeded to write some notes in a file that was opened up on the desk in the corner of the room. I then explained that the main purpose of my visit was to have him look at a strange spot of my face. When he heard my question, he spun around quickly and asked me where the spot was. I pointed it out to him and before I realized what was happening, he was spraying the spot with something. Well that something turned out to be liquid nitrogen. It stung a bit, and he quickly explained to me that he had killed the skin in that area and that I could expect some excessive flaking in that area. He then put down his canister of liquid nitrogen and proceeded out of the room. He had been in the room for no more than ninety seconds. I felt somewhat violated and I wasn't exactly sure why.

Quite Staggering

Running the house also means making sure that the proper people come out to the house to keep things in order. There is the exterminator to keep the bugs at bay. Then there is the septic pump guy. His job is very important since we like it when the poop goes down the toilet. There is the guy who comes out every year to replace the ultraviolet light bulb so the bacteria cannot get into the house. The lawn care guys come out to fertilize and keep the lawn lush and green.

(I used to do this myself but when I ran the numbers to determine how much it cost me to do the work, I figured out that they do it at the same cost. I am no idiot so I hired them to do it). Once every two years we get the driveway sealed. Once again, they can do it cheaper than I can. The chimney gets swept once a year. The oil deliveries come regularly. The oil heater and hot water heater get serviced once a year. It is staggering to reflect on what it takes to keep the house properly maintained.

Chapter 14

Gather Around the Campfire

Great Memories from a Great Organization

Boy Scouts is a great organization. I have been involved in the program as a boy as well as an adult for over twenty years. The times spent with fellow scouts have yielded some of the best memories I have. It is hard to recall how many times I have laughed until I cried, stood there in awe of Mother Nature, realized the significance of an accomplishment, or learned a valuable lesson from interacting with one of the boys. There are too many to count. However, I wanted to try and share some of these great memories.

Attitude is Everything

When Ryan joined his first Boy Scout troop, it seemed to rain on every outdoor activity we attended. It was no exception during the World War II Re-enactment and Air Show that we attended in Reading, Pennsylvania. It was raining hard on the drive to the campground that Friday evening. The boys were full of nervous energy and I wanted to make sure they had a memorable time. We spent the three-hour trip singing songs, playing games, and telling jokes. It was a genuine good time. At that moment, I did not know it, but the tone for the weekend had been established. We arrived at camp and set up the tents in the dark while it was raining.

No one complained. The troop had adopted the philosophy that the poor weather was the "cards we had been dealt," and we did the best we could.

The next day it was still raining and raining hard. One of the patrols was forced to cook breakfast out in the rain since we did not have enough tarps to provide cover for every patrol. The members of the patrol did not mind at all as they stood there cooking their breakfast and laughing the whole time. After breakfast, we went to the air show. It was an amazing display with all of the vintage planes from World War II. None of the planes were flying due to the poor conditions. The re-enactors were camping in their vintage canvas tents and from the looks of it were not very dry. In fact, it was quite apparent that they were soaking wet. The relentless rains kept coming and coming. The water was up to several inches deep since the ground was saturated and the water had nowhere to go. When the rains got torrential, we would hang out under one of the wings of the planes and just laugh. It rained the whole weekend and I had one of the best times of my life. I learned a huge lesson during that trip. The experience of life is dictated by your attitude and outlook. Control the things you can and live with the rest.

Here are the boys waiting out the storm

The Trials of Travel

Getting to the camping trips was sometimes arduous. The typical destination was three hours away. Our troop believed that this distance discouraged parents from coming to get their sons during the camping trip and taking them back for a soccer game or other activity. For the most part it worked, but it also led to some exciting traveling adventures. For instance, there was the trip to the C&O Canal which runs along the Potomac River. Before I tell you this story, I need to let you know that one adult was in charge of obtaining directions for all of the drivers to get to the campground. These directions came from one of the many on-line computer services available. Just as usual, the directions were distributed and everyone headed off.

On this particular trip, we were about two and a half hours into it and close to our final destination. The drivers were tired and the kids' energy levels were dropping as well. That is when it happened. The road appeared to end, but the directions said to continue straight ahead. We pressed forward cautiously and, sure enough, there was a gravel road that began at the dark edge of the forest. The drivers discussed it and decided to continue. The road got narrower and narrower as we proceeded. The road also went downhill at a rather steep angle. We got to a point where turning around was no longer a viable option so we continued to press forward. The Scoutmaster, who was in the lead vehicle, came over the two-way radios that each driver had and told us that he thought there was a good possibility of there being a river at the bottom of the hill. Several minutes passed by and then he came on the radio again and said that there indeed was a river. This was no dry river bed or a small trickling stream. It was about twenty feet wide and about a foot deep. All of us decided to proceed, except the one driver who was in his tiny Miata which was only about eight inches off the ground and weighed next to nothing. He was afraid that the current would take him away.

I was a bit skeptical at this point but my overriding urge was to get to the campsite and set up camp. I proceeded with great caution in the minivan, which is not really designed to traverse boulder-filled streams. I was relieved when I had successfully crossed. While I was crossing, I could not help but notice the red tail lights of the vehicles in front of me that appeared to be taking flight as they turned left and started to ascend the very steep hill in front of us. At the top of the hill there was a field (sort of) where we reassessed our situation. The road was getting worse, so we decided to turn around. Upon reflection, I realize that my minivan has crossed a significant stream not once, but twice!

Ahh, the Joys of the Great Outdoors

Sleeping on the ground without climate control can create its own set of issues. The adults had tent buddies just like the boys. This was more for sharing in the misery than for safety reasons. Being an adult and trying to minimize the misery, we are always looking for brilliant ideas that will lead to a good night's sleep. Some of the adults use portable air mattresses which provide a nice cushion to sleep on. However, you just have to know what you are doing ... Case in point is one trip when an adult was blowing up his air mattress late one night. He was having real problems blowing it up, and once he pulled his lips away from the nozzle, the air would all rush out. After struggling with this for about ten minutes, it dawned on him that he was actually sitting on the air mattress which a) did not allow air to get in and b) caused any air in the mattress to come rushing out. His discovery caused him to laugh uncontrollably and when one of the other adults in an adjacent tent asked him to keep it down, he burst out laughing even harder!

Temperature was also sometimes an issue when it came to sleeping. I recall one trip to Assateague Island, which is a beach camping experience. It is always unique. Sometimes there are gale force winds, which carry tents away across the dunes, and other times there are more bugs than you can imagine. This one particular trip it was the heat that was the challenge. Being hot during the day was one thing, but being hot at night creates a different set of issues. I clearly remember laying there in the tent that hot sticky night. First, I was in the sleeping bag, then in the sleeping bag with it unzipped, then on top of the sleeping bag, and finally, stripped down to my underwear on top of the sleeping bag. I spent most of the night listening to my tent buddies sighing and wondering when the morning would come. It did finally come, but when it did, we were quite exhausted. Of course, there is the other temperature extreme ...

The one instance that comes to mind was a cabin experience in January. I use the term "cabin" loosely since you could see outside from the inside through the cracks between the boards in the walls. I had a sleeping bag which was woefully inadequate. I spent the entire night wondering if I would survive. When I got up in the morning I called home. I asked Michele to go over to our home thermometer and hit the "low" button which gives the lowest temperature reading. I knew that the old record was four degrees. When I asked her what it read, she said, "one." Take my word for it...people should not camp in an inadequate sleeping bag when the temperature is "one."

<u>You Just Have to Laugh</u>

Modern technology plays a part in Boy Scouts just like it does in all parts of our lives. We were traveling to a summer camp experience in Halliburton, Canada which is in the middle of nowhere. The Scoutmaster was driving and decided to activate the satellite telephone hardwired into his

SUV since cell phones would be inoperable at camp. This was a great idea, but he hadn't read the owner's manual on how to operate the phone, so we were learning as we went. The system is voice activated for the most part where a kind lady asks you questions that allow you to make the calls. It turns out that we were proficient in making calls. It was ending calls that caused all of the problems. We had just finished a call and we could hear the person on the other end of the line hanging up. There was no physical phone to hang up on our end so we tried to say the command 'hang up.' This did not work. We tried saying 'end call' when the lady came on the line and asked us what we wanted to do. We said it again and she proceeded to tell us that she would dial that number. We protested, but she dialed it anyway. The person on the other end picked up the phone. It was the person that we had just been talking to! We laughed and told her of our dilemma. We then said goodbye, heard her hang up, and proceeded to try and hang up on our end. We tried 'stop,' 'please stop,' 'end,' 'finish,' 'close' and all sorts of other voice commands. Most of the time the kind lady would come on and say she would be happy to dial that number for us. She would also ask us to speak more slowly, which we did, but to no avail. After a while we were howling with laughter. Three grown men could not figure out how to hang up the phone!

Plenty of Food & Drink

Food is definitely one of the highlights of any Boy Scout camping trip. It provides comfort and energy to get through that day's activities. A typical breakfast is bacon followed by pancakes with some juice and milk. One morning the boys were all busy preparing breakfast. The Scoutmaster would occasionally check on the boys to see how they were doing and provide any helpful guidance. He checked on the first patrol and they had completed the meal and were beginning to clean up. The second and third patrols were also cleaning up. He was a bit surprised when he got to the fourth patrol and found that they were still cooking their bacon. He asked the group of four boys what the problem was because he knew they had been busy the entire morning. They said that there was no problem and everything was running smoothly. The Scoutmaster then had a realization and asked *how much* bacon they were cooking. He was flabbergasted when they told him they were cooking three pounds of bacon! It came as no surprise that their patrol cheer became "Bears! Bears! We like bacon! We like bacon cuz bacon is good!"

Dehydration is an important condition to be on the lookout for during all scout functions. Now that I look back, I am pretty sure that I spent my entire childhood dehydrated. It was rare back then to catch me taking a drink of water. Some things never change, which I have noticed on numerous occasions since I have been an adult leader. It has been very typical for a scout, especially the younger scouts, to come up and tell me they were tired or had a headache. I would ask them if they had been drinking throughout the day. They would insist that they had. Upon asking them how much they had to drink, they would produce an eight-ounce bottle half full and say "Look at all I drank!!" I always tried to explain to them that they needed to drink a lot more than that. They usually insisted that they were not dehydrated, but when I sat them down in the shade and gave them some water, they always rebounded in fifteen to thirty minutes. They never admitted to possibly being dehydrated, but I can only hope they will remember next time.

<u>Excellent Trip & Pre-Planning</u>

Then there was the trip to downtown Washington, DC which had been planned by my son Ryan. He did an excellent job planning the trip which included taking the

Metro train into the downtown area. Overall, the trip was great, but keeping everyone together was challenging. When we arrived in the city, it was decided that each group would be free to do what they wanted and that we would rendezvous at 4:00 that afternoon. Each adult had six to eight boys in their group. After the day was over, several adults shared with me that keeping track of the boys assigned to their group was like herding cats and they were surprised that they had not lost any of them.

The other challenge was getting back out of the city. Initially, we got onto the Metro with no problems. The train appeared to be filled to capacity. About halfway out of the city, however, the Metro unexpectedly stopped and the conductor came over the P.A. system and told us we had to disembark and catch the next train. There were about forty of us, and we watched in horror as each preceding train came into the station at capacity. The fear was that we could be there all day waiting for a train empty enough to accommodate all of us. A collective decision was then made to "cram" onto the next train. The next train arrived and it was like a panicked event as the adults threw the boys onto the train in a hurried fashion since the doors are only open for so long. Surprisingly enough, we did not lose anyone.

A similar event happened in the Cub Scouts. A bus trip was planned to go to New York City about a month before Christmas. The crowds were amazing! It was the first time that I experienced "pedestrian gridlock." Anyway, each family was given the liberty to go where they wanted as long as they came back to the bus by 6:00 that evening at the Rockefeller Center. Our family had a wonderful time and got to see the Statue of Liberty as well as some of the other sites in the city. We faithfully arrived at Rockefeller Center at 6:00 but forgot how big it is! It took ten minutes or so to locate our bus, but we got on safely. Some of the other families were less fortunate. Unbeknownst to them, the bus could only park there for approximately fifteen minutes before being asked to move. When the last family had not shown up, the bus driver had no choice but to pull out and wander around the gridlocked streets of New York City. It was terrible. We couldn't contact the missing family since they did not have a cell phone. We wandered around for a while but not before the bus driver got into a minor fender bender. The family was finally located, but the bus driver would not stop for dinner on the way home since his schedule was ruined!

Plans are Made to be Changed

I have learned that plans are made to be changed. This has been a very valuable lesson learned through Boy Scouts. I was once in charge of planning a bike hike. After doing extensive research on the Greater Allegheny Passage, which is essentially an extension of the Chesapeake & Ohio Canal trail from Cumberland, Maryland up to Pittsburgh, Pennsylvania, I found a bike hike that would allow the younger scouts to be challenged as well as provide a longer ride for the older boys so they would be challenged as well. I was very proud of myself and the trip I put together until that Saturday when we got ready to leave. It was raining relatively hard and riding your bike on a muddy trail while it is raining is difficult and sometimes dangerous. Also some of the boys had forgotten to bring their rain gear so they could not go, at least not right away. As the rain continued that morning the trip kept getting adjusted to Plan B and then Plan C since we were losing the window of time available to ride. We also successfully found an alternate activity for the boys who forgot to bring their rain gear. When the rains finally subsided and when we finally executed our plan, we were literally on Plan G.

Feeling your Senses Come Alive

Being involved with Boy Scouts involves all of the senses. The organization has allowed me to experience the sense of touch ... like when I sat beneath the waterfall from a mountain spring and felt the 30-degree water cascade over my shoulders, or when I hiked up and down mountains and felt the burn in my muscles, or when I stood out in the sun and felt the warmth on my skin. The Boy Scout program has allowed me to smell wonderful things ... like the smell of coffee on a cold winter day, the smell of saltwater at the beach, or the smell of turkey and stuffing cooking at the January cabin retreat. My involvement has allowed me to hear many wonderful things ... like the cry of an eagle or the words of encouragement that an older scout provides to a younger scout. It has allowed me to taste many interesting things ... like a patrol's entry in a cooking competition or a drink of cold water after a long hike. And as far as sight ... I have seen secluded waterfalls, natural pools of warm water suitable for swimming, endless forests, pristine waters, bubbling pools of mud, and glorious mountains.

One of the most amazing things I ever witnessed was seeing the Grand Tetons mountain range. We first spotted them from the plane when we were flying to Wyoming for a western summer camp experience. They are peculiar in that they kind of erupt out of the ground from nowhere. They are even more impressive when you are standing in front of them. They remind me of the Matterhorn Mountains in Switzerland. The difference from the bottom of the Grand Teton mountain range to the top is over two miles, and it is something I will never forget.

The Wide Array of Opportunities

Boy Scouts offers many opportunities to experience new things and to challenge yourself. I have canoed, camped for many consecutive nights in a tent, climbed poles, white water rafted, swum in 56-degree water, lifeguarded at the ocean, built campfires, cooked on a portable stove, participated in numerous conservation projects, served as a merit badge counselor working with hundreds of boys, skied down mountains, oriented a map, tied thousands of knots, fished, shot a black powder rifle, tossed tomahawks, and biked and hiked just to name some of the things. As an adult, I have been challenged numerous times, and I am happy to have met those challenges. I have backpacked seventeen miles in a single day a couple of times. I have biked fifty miles in a single day as a requirement for the Bicycling Merit Badge. I have also climbed to the top of a mountain over two miles high.

Most Impressive of All

By far, the most impressive part of the Scouting program is the boys themselves. They never cease to amaze me. There was the time the troop went on an eight-mile hike along the Appalachian Trail. (For those of you who are not familiar with the trail, it is sometimes arduous with many uphill climbs and downhill descents). There were tons of rocks on that particular stretch of the trail, and if you weren't paying attention, you were likely to fall flat on your face. One of the primary focuses of the troop is having the adults encourage the older scouts to work with the younger scouts to motivate them to succeed. On the eight-mile hike that day, an older boy by the name of Tim took it upon himself to hang out in the rear of the group to assist any of the younger scouts. He did a great job for the full eight hours on the trail. He worked with one particular young scout who started to really struggle about halfway through the hike. With Tim's encouragement, the younger scout was able to complete that day's hike and have a real sense of accomplishment.

Then there was another scout who was experiencing the Appalachian Trail for the first time. He had borrowed a backpack which was a little bit too big for him, but he somehow made it through the day. At the end of the day, I helped him remove his pack. I was surprised to feel how heavy it was. I asked him to show me what was in his pack. He began to unpack and showed me how he had brought an extra pair of shoes (not needed and quite heavy), his scout book (not needed and quite heavy) and a huge can of Dinty Moore Stew (needed but inappropriate). No wonder he had been struggling all day! I made a mental note to check all of the younger scouts' backpacks before another trip such as this.

Then there was Jonathan. He was one of those quiet scouts who eventually became the troop's Senior Patrol Leader. The Senior Patrol Leader is the top leadership position within the troop. He did a great job in this role. He led by example. He always had an upbeat disposition. He was able to get those around him to accomplish the tasks at hand while making it fun at the same time. He was an expert in working with people including the adults. We saw him time and again listen to what someone had to say, no matter how rude or ridiculous, and either implement it without complaint or diffuse it without insulting that person. The adult leaders were amazed and started to take his lead on how to handle these situations. In situations such as this, I find that it is typical for me to be inspired by the boys.

Then there was Jonathan's best friend Travis. Travis was another quiet scout who hung out in the background for most of the early part of his Scouting career. One day the adult leaders were discussing various scouts in the troop and Travis' name came up. We knew he was one of the older and more responsible boys in the troop, so we assumed he was a higher rank. Someone asked him what his rank was and he said Second Class, which is only the second rank in Boy Scouts. We were shocked! We knew that the younger boys looked up to him and he provided leadership and guidance with little or no effort. He was very effective in the role of a leader. I thought of him as Eagle Scout material, but by the time we realized this dilemma, it was too late. He was almost eighteen, and Scouting rules only allow scouts to reach their Eagle rank if they do so before age eighteen. He stayed with the troop until he went off to college. I admire him to this day. He was recognized as "Scout of the Year" for all of his efforts, a title which he truly deserved.

Then there was my experience with Conrad. I perceive that Conrad had trouble believing he could accomplish things. The Scouting program showed him that he could. On his first summer camp experience, it was learned that he was a beginner swimmer. He was not really comfortable in the water and did not really want to learn. The adult leaders talked to some of the camp staff members and explained the situation. They agreed to work with him and by the end of the week he was swimming across the entire pool. His confidence swelled.

A True Gift in Return

I have worked with hundreds of boys and have enjoyed it all -- whether it was planning a trip with one of them, conducting advancement reviews, working with the older scouts in the troop, encouraging the boy leaders, being a merit badge counselor, or just sitting down once a year to see how they were doing. It has truly been an honor every time I work with the boys. I truly believe that I am sometimes taking more than I am giving. There have been numerous instances where a boy will tell me something about leadership, his values, his ease in public speaking, or what his hopes and goals are. Sometimes the conversations are way beyond their years. The boys truly inspire me.

I remember one specific time when a boy discussed with me his readiness to meet with the Scoutmaster regarding his advancement to Star Rank. We called these meetings Assistant Scoutmaster reviews. Leadership is a component of the Star Rank. Anyway, I knew he held the leadership position of Bugler for the Troop. He shared with me that he had attended four of the last six camping trips but forgot his bugle on two of them. He then sat back and thought about what he had just said. Without any prompting from me, he came to the conclusion that this was not truly active leadership and he was not ready for Star Rank. He and I then developed a plan with leadership goals that he should strive for. I was extremely proud of him at that moment.

Roles of the Boys and Adults

Our troop is truly "boy led." The adults are there to provide guidance and ensure that everything the troop does is safe. The boys are primarily in charge of planning what trips we will be attending, what we will be doing on the trips, and planning the weekly troop meetings. It is very impressive. That is why I believe most of our boys stayed involved with the troop until they were eighteen years old because the environment is exciting and cultivating. Many of the scouts even went on to become adult leaders in the troop. I have had several instances in which total strangers have come up to me during one of our troop functions and said how impressed they were with how our troop was run. They said that our troop "got it," meaning that the boys were in charge and doing a wonderful job. To me that was the greatest compliment our troop could receive.

I hope it is obvious that Boy Scouting is an organization that I really believe in. I have given until it hurts and I don't mind. I am not in it for selfish reasons. I am in it to hopefully make a positive difference in a boy's life. If I am truly honest, I would have to admit that I am trying to have half the impact on a boy in our troop that my Scoutmaster had on me when I was a young man. Sometimes I find myself wondering if that is the kind of impact I am making, and then a parent will share with me how much they appreciate my efforts in working with their son and keeping him on track. Those moments are priceless. They are priceless because that is not my goal; it is simply icing on the cake to get any acknowledgement for the work that I have done.

I would not trade my efforts in the Scouting program for <u>all</u> of the money in the world.

Chapter 15

Carline

Plenty of New Horizons

As Mr. Mom, I was expected to do a lot of things for our family that I had not done in the past. In other words, now that I had the time, it was time to fill it! Some of these things were mundane and others were ... well, ***not*** mundane. One of the more interesting things I participated in was fondly known as "carline."

Our daughter was attending the school associated with our church. It was a wonderful experience for her but created several additional tasks for us as a family. One of them was carline. "What is carline," you might ask? If I were to define it in the simplest terms possible, I would say that "Carline is the method through which kids were dropped off and picked up from school." If only it were that easy ... The need for carline arose from the fact that there were no buses that went to the school and the school itself was very isolated. Therefore, every student had to be driven to school as well as picked up.

The Process

The carline process itself was very organized. It had to be revised every year as the school grew and the need for more space and efficiency was required. Upon arrival at 7:30 a.m., I queued up into a single lane through the church's parking lot along a specific route. (As background, a sketch of the route was provided to each family at the beginning of every school year). Occasionally, people would not follow the required route and that would throw the whole system into a tailspin. Recovery from a debacle such as this could only occur through people's good will and patience.

While waiting in line, I got to inspect the occupants of the other cars and would find a rather eclectic mix. Some parents were all spiffy as they were dressed to go to work, while others had obviously just rolled out of bed and were trying hard not to make eye contact with the other drivers waiting in line. I would drive up to the drop-off spot, a ten-foot section along the curb break in front of the door, and let Danielle off. I could not drop her off before reaching this designated area for reasons that I am still not sure of today. Either our priest or the school principal would be there to greet the children as they got out of the cars. Sometimes they would open the car doors for the kids, and it was amusing to watch them as they tried to figure out how to shut the doors, especially on the cars with automatic closing features. Several times I had to pull over after dropping off Danielle to shut my van door which both of them obviously thought had the automatic closing feature. (It did not).

It was the afternoon pick-up that was ***much*** more interesting. Many parents would arrive before the designated 2:45 p.m. pick-up time. The idea was the earlier you got there, the quicker you could get your child and get on to other things. Also, by arriving early, parents would "take care of business." For this, they would get out of their cars and talk to other parents. From what I gathered, they would talk about the upcoming fundraisers, discuss their vacation plans, or unload craft supplies from one car to the other. It was like this little culture would materialize every afternoon right there in the church parking lot from 2:30 to 2:45. The only drawback is that I was not a part of this culture. It's probably because I was one of the only fathers there. I have to admit that I felt somewhat excluded, but I made good use of the time by doing paperwork, writing letters, and reading novels.

Of course, there was a procedure associated with the pick-up. First there was the arrival. For the pick-up, it was not a single line like it was in the morning. Rather, it was a dual line down the aisle closest to the school and then a single line proceeding after that. I had a name card for Danielle that I put in the windshield of the car. That was so the carline administrative person could write down Danielle's name in the proper spot on the check-in sheet. That sheet would then be taken into the school and the kids' names would be read over the P.A. system. At that point, the kids would come out of the school in the order the cars were queued in the parking lot. The kids would then wait along the curb and proceed to the cars only when told to do so. Once given the command, they would get into their respective car and drive off. Does this sound complex? It was a bit complex, and as a result, it did not always work. I would say nine times out of ten it worked well. The times it did not work well would be when I was sitting there in my car and Danielle would not be one of the students in the group who had just come out of the school. I would then have to drive off without her and park the car and talk to the carline administrative person who would then go off to find her.

All in all, the carline process consumed about forty-five minutes of my day. I tried to make the best of that time, but that got me wondering how the parents in the situation where both worked made carline work ...

Chapter 16

Rearing

Feeling Blessed

My greatest blessing is my family. Michele and I were fortunate to have two very healthy children. Ryan is one of the most social people I know and has many characteristics of a natural born leader. Danielle has many talents including art and music. She is also very funny but doesn't think so. Both do well at school and take their studies seriously.

A great moment with the kids

I remember when Ryan was born. There we were holding a newborn child and all I kept thinking is, "Wow, I hope I don't screw this up! " (I used to always kid Michele and ask where the kid owners' manual was). It was then that I started to reflect on the child rearing techniques that I saw my parents use and began to apply them to my own family. Looking back, I would have to say that we did a decent job of bringing up our kids. Being at home for seven years allowed me a greater opportunity to interact with both children and to help build a solid foundation of values for them.

I have always tried to get involved at some level in all of the kids' activities. They say that children are more likely to be successful if their parents play some role in the various aspects of their lives. I believe this occurs because my children see me consuming my time and energy, and I have a stake in what is going on in their lives. I also believe that my involvement allows me to fully understand what they are doing. Otherwise my understanding would be much more limited, since my kids typically give single-word responses like "good" when I ask how things are going in their various clubs and teams. With responses like that, I would know virtually nothing about what is going on in their lives! Now I have to admit that some activities I get involved with significantly and others not quite so much. I did learn that by being involved, I get to experience their lives firsthand and also have fun. It is rewarding for me to interact with younger people, to learn what is going on in their lives, and to provide guidance when the opportunity arises. Being involved also keeps me busy.

Some Trial and Error

I find it best to limit both Ryan's and Danielle's involvement to three clubs, teams and/or organizations each at any one given time. On the one hand, Michele and I have always wanted our kids to experience many different types of activities so they can "try them on and see if they fit." However, there is a fine line between cultivating a healthy dose of culture and throwing our lives into total chaos. After some trial and error, I found that three activities for each child worked best for our family.

This philosophy of three activities for each child usually meant that there was one kid activity each night of the week, and on those nights when there were two, Michele and I would have to use the "divide and conquer" approach. There were times when our lives seemed to be getting out of control. Nine times out of ten, when I would count how many activities the kids were in, they were in five or six each and we would have to decide which ones we were going to have to cut back. One last point and then I will move on. I realized I had to be careful about direct contact with my children during any activity. I would intentionally try not to directly interact with them too much so that they could just be themselves. I remember going on a Boy Scout trip for a week-long adventure out west to Yellowstone National Park and the Grand Tetons. We went as a family and did not see Ryan for almost the entire trip. We actually "adopted" another boy whose parents could not attend. The point is that everyone had a great time and Ryan's independence was stretched.

Try this on for Size

One of the fun things about having kids is that we get to have an agenda and gently push our values onto them. This is true with everything from religion to what we consider good music. I remember purchasing the DVD featuring the first volume of the Looney Tunes Golden Collection. (For those of you who do not know what Looney Tunes are, although I find that hard to believe, I will explain). Looney Tunes are the cartoons featuring various characters developed by the Warner Brothers studio. The cartoons featured many awesome characters including Bugs Bunny, Yosemite Sam, Sylvester the Cat, Tweety Bird, Granny, the Road Runner and Coyote, Sam the Sheepdog, the Tasmanian Devil, Marvin the Martian, Foghorn Leghorn, Henery Hawk, Speedy Gonzales, Elmer Fudd, Pepe Le Pew, Porky Pig, Petunia Pig, and my favorite: Daffy Duck. Many of these were directed by the infamous Fritz Fleming and Chuck Jones. Voices were done by the true voiceover genius Mel

Blanc. Who else could do a voice of Bugs Bunny impersonating Daffy Duck and make it work? I clearly recall when I was a kid watching this zany cast of characters every Saturday morning. They would cause each other all kinds of pain, and my brother and I would laugh until we cried.

Knowing what a role these cartoons played in my childhood, I wanted to pass the fun onto my children. When Ryan and Danielle were old enough, I would play these cartoons for them while they ate breakfast before heading off to school. We would rank each cartoon on a scale of 1 to 5, with 5 as the best. I have to admit that there were a lot more 1's than I care to remember. However, the cool part of the experience was that I was able to show them something that I enjoyed as a kid and pass that onto them.

<u>One of my Many Blessings</u>

Both Ryan and Danielle have taken their schoolwork very seriously, and this is a true blessing. When they came home from school, they always sat down to do their homework before doing anything else. Michele and I never forced them to do it. They did it on their own. Ryan would always go up to his room to do his homework while Danielle would stay in our family room to do hers. I would always make it a point to be inside when Danielle would arrive home from school. I would go through the mail while she began her homework. She did not know it at the time, but it was a regular highlight of my day. I looked forward to her coming home asking her how her day went and maybe even guiding her through some of her homework. She would ask me to read some of her books to her or help her study for a test. I always enjoyed it. Not only was I learning more about things such as the men who signed the Declaration of Independence or the Pythagorean Theorem, but I was also interacting with Danielle on a very positive level. It was what I like to call a "win- win" situation.

Nerve-wracking, to Say the Least

I find that there are many times we get to teach our kids necessary skills that can be quite intimidating. I have shown my kids how to use various tools, how to change a car tire, and how to start a fire. However, one of the most daunting skills that I had to teach them was how to drive. It is one of the most helpless and hopeless experiences that I have ever had to live through. It is really crazy when I sit down to think about it. We are expected to throw our keys to our teenagers and tell them that today is that special day when they learn how to drive. They slide into the driver's seat behind the steering wheel of a two-ton piece of metal that has the capability of wreaking all kinds of havoc if things go wrong. Then I, as the parent, sit in the passenger's seat where I have absolutely no control over what is about to happen. All I can do is say things like "slow down" or "the brake is the pedal on the right." I have to try to say it calmly in a way that doesn't frighten them and make them do something even more dangerous.

I clearly remember telling Ryan that he was driving too close to the center line of the roadway. However, instead of taking my advice, he saw this as an opportunity to have a discussion as to why he felt he was not too close to the center line. I tried to calmly explain that driving too close would put him closer to the opposing traffic and possibly result in a head-on collision. He did not see it that way and stuck to his guns. I mean, he did already have twelve hours of driving under his belt (compared to my thirty years' worth), so why shouldn't I trust his judgment?!? I could not take it, so Michele did all of the driving lessons after that incident. I must have aged a decade in the first year of his driving. I cannot wait until Danielle starts...

Is this where the love of cars begins?

Sharing Traditions & Holidays Together

Family traditions are important. I believe that we are all creatures of habit. If we create an environment of healthy habits, I believe that our children will embrace them and carry them throughout their lives. These traditions can be simple and yet still effective. One example is eating dinner together every day and saying a prayer at the beginning of the meal. It is important to me that there is that daily connection with each other as a family. The conversation may not be uplifting and meaningful at each meal, but there will be times when it is. I clearly remember meals with my family when I was a teenager. We would share scenes from a favorite funny movie that we had enjoyed together. We would recite the scenes line-for-line and then laugh until we cried! I believe prayer at mealtime is also important. Having an open communication with God allows us to be thankful for the many blessings in our lives and to keep those in mind who may be struggling.

Another family tradition is to make sure we take regular family outings which create lasting memories. We go to Hershey Park, Pennsylvania, every summer for a day. The types of rides the kids enjoy has changed over the years, but the fact that we do it together as a family has not. It is one tradition that I have enjoyed tremendously.

Twisted Traditions can be Fun

Halloween has always been one of our favorite holidays with lots of family traditions. We fully decorate the inside of our house with pumpkins, hanging spiders, vampires, skeletons, and other various Halloween garb. The outside of the house is where we really have fun. I built a huge spider web made out of string and hung it over the front of our house. It was probably about ten feet wide and twenty feet tall. We built a giant spider about three feet long and four feet wide and hung it in the web. It looked lonely up there on the web all by itself, so one year, I added a baby doll wrapped in cotton to make it look like the spider had cocooned her and was ready to eat her. I set up a spotlight on it so it could be seen throughout the night. An added benefit is that the light casts scary shadows up onto the house. It is quite a production to hang the web every year and takes a couple of hours.

One year I decided not to hang it and I was asked numerous times by our neighbors where it was. It was then that I decided that I needed to hang it every year. It was also then that I decided to ask the kids to help me put it up!

Our spider was a hit!

We also constructed the Haunted Woods, which was a gravel pathway through the woods between our house and our neighbor's house. We set up tiki torches to light the way. We hung severed arms from the trees along with flying bats. We set up an area that looked like a fresh grave was being dug. We hooked up strobe lights, sound machines, fog machines, and ... well, you get the idea. It was something we did as a family and we loved the reactions we would get from kids who made the jaunt through the woods. For some of the older kids we made it even more "special" by hiding out in the woods and jumping out to scare them. It was truly twisted!

Camp Dad

Summertime posed a new twist in our lives now that I was a stay-at-home dad. In the past, the kids would typically attend numerous summer camps and we would go on a family vacation. Now that I was staying at home, I decided that they would go to fewer camps, which would save a little money, and they would now go to "Camp Dad." It was a great opportunity for me to interact with them and teach them some values and responsibility. And there was the fun side of things, too. We would make crafts like placemats made with pictures of our family. We would go the local park to hang out. I helped Danielle start a small company where she built bulletin boards made out of corks and then sold them. We would sometimes watch a good movie, hang out in the hot tub, or have a video game tournament. Ryan and I volunteered at our church's Vacation Bible Camp together. We went hiking on some of the local trails.

Posing for my new adventure ahead as a Counselor for Vacation Bible School

Then there were the badminton tournaments held in our backyard where the neighborhood kids would come and play. We would go to visit people who had pools and have a relaxing day in the sun. We shot off rockets, pulled together baseball games at the local park, and played putt-putt golf at the local golf course. We also played basketball in our driveway as well as stick ball. There were many, many board games that we played. Some of our favorites were Trouble, Twister, Dominos, Chinese Checkers, Jenga, Rebound, Catch Phrase, and Life, to name just a few. We played darts and read together. We went to the library and the local nature center. I would take the kids to play dates and they would invite their friends over to our house as well. We visited one of our friend's alpaca which lived at a local farm. I also took the opportunity to teach various skills to the kids. We worked on maintaining the cars, painting various parts of the house, building pieces of furniture, running errands, grocery shopping, gardening, remodeling our kitchen, cleaning the house, cutting the lawn ... It was an incredible opportunity for them as well as for me.

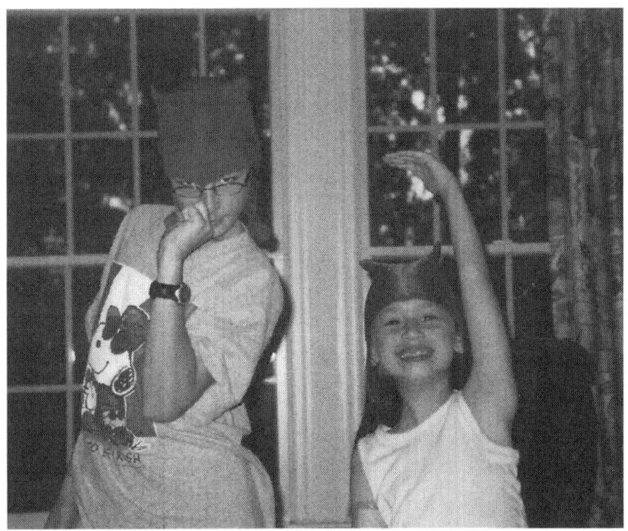

Once again, the kids acting goofy ...

<u>Taking Advantage of Opportunities</u>

Opportunities are there every day of our lives. It is my opinion that we need to look for them and be open to them. I also believe that even simply trying to lead a good life provides a strong example for others and has a positive influence on them. An example of this is Michele and I have always taken a strong stand in supporting healthy relationships including the institution of marriage. Our relationship is not perfect, since I believe there is no such thing. However, we do not belittle each other in public, and we would encourage others to do the same. We get politically involved with issues regarding marriage and we "put our money where our mouth is" by getting involved with Marriage Encounter, an organization that makes good marriages better. We make our relationship a priority.

Every year we plan an anniversary celebration. We alternate who plans that year's celebration. It is fun to plan a trip, but it is also fun to not know where you are going until the day arrives. I know our kids are watching us and taking mental notes. Keeping it fresh, not taking each other for granted, and having respect for each other are just some of the values that I hope our kids take with them into their own relationships.

Michele and I enjoying a dinner with just the two of us

Chapter 17

Where's the Elevator?

Finding Myself on the Stage Crew

As I have said before, I am a firm believer in volunteering. It's fun, but more importantly, it's what makes life interesting and full of opportunities that I wouldn't have experienced otherwise.

My daughter Danielle is our "artistic child." She has my wife and I running her to piano lessons, dance recitals, choir rehearsals, art classes and of course, the local plays. She has been in so many plays that I am not sure what the total count is. I have learned that having your child in a play is not as simple as it sounds. I guess I originally expected that she would have to memorize some lines, sing some songs, and attend practices so that she would know where to stand and when. That, my friends, is just the tip of a very large iceberg. The parents have to get involved so the play is a total success. There is the set construction, costume development, prop construction, lighting set-up, sound, publicity, tee shirts for the players and crew, concessions, fundraising, program production, musical production, snacks, and of course, the stage crew. That's where I come in.

I remember when I first volunteered to serve on the set construction crew. I thought to myself, "How hard can this be?" I mean, it's just the local community children's theatre. What I didn't realize was that I was embarking upon a great adventure. If I had been told all of the things I would do prior to my commitment, I would have thought it over a little bit longer.

Getting Clued In

My first clue that this was a large task was that there was a schedule associated with the efforts of the set construction crew. It was long and complex. We would get together two or three nights a week every week for months leading up to the play. Over the years, I have helped to build chariots, shipwrecks, elephants, caves, wardrobes, palaces, sheer curtains, flyovers, temples, boats, hovering tables, and the list goes on and on. Another highly demanded item we always seemed to be building were additional stage sections. The plays were held in the local high school auditorium and the director's vision always included that the stage be tiered with two and sometimes three levels. Also, it was deemed that the auditorium stage was not big enough, so we always extended the stage out towards the audience. We probably built several new sections of stage for each new production and assembled a total of fifteen to twenty of them. It was a huge effort, and I was beginning to see how the set crews of Broadway shows must feel.

Talk about Anxiety!

The additional stage sections were easy to construct and had a relatively simple design. Two-by-fours and plywood were used to build the four-foot-by-eight-foot deck as well as the legs. The highest platforms were about three to four feet in the air. Having an engineering background always caused me to have anxiety about everything we constructed. It was all very flimsy because nothing was considered to be "permanent." These elevated stage sections definitely fit into the category of flimsy, and when I considered the number of cast members that would be standing on them at any given time, I would feel a little queasy.

The lighting for the production was just as detailed as the rest of the show. The lights that were already in the high school auditorium were considered to be inadequate so additional lights were rented. During set up it would be the set crew's job to take down the existing lights and install the new ones. I get goose bumps just thinking about how hard it was to take down the existing lights. You see, you couldn't use a ladder for this task since it was a two-man job and the lights were about fifteen feet in the air. The existing lights were a single unit that consisted of six individual lights. Each unit was six to eight feet long and I would guess weighed about 150 pounds. It was suspended by chains. So the procedure to remove the existing lights would go something like this: Two men would climb on top of one of the elevated stage sections that had boxes stacked on top of them. One man would then grab the unit of lights, lift it into the air, unhook the chain, rest the unit on his shoulder, and then wait for the other man to do the same thing on the other side of the unit. All of this was done while precariously swaying. I thought we were going to die.

The stories about the ladders we used for set up were just as unnerving. We would climb ladders as high as forty feet in the air to attach pulleys on the ceiling so the sheer curtains and flyovers could be lowered when needed. We used some A-frame ladders that were just gargantuan. There is nothing quite like the sensation of swaying while at the top of a huge ladder. It was not for the faint of heart.

The Elephant in the Room

Some of the set pieces we built were quite impressive as well as scary. One of my favorite recollections was the elephant that was needed for one scene. We were instructed that the elephant had to be able to accommodate one of the actors on top and actually look like an elephant. So the set crew collectively brainstormed on how we should do this. We assumed that the elephant had to be stored outside the auditorium in a hallway so it would not be a distraction to the audience. Therefore, it had to fit through the door that led into the auditorium. Using that assumption, we began building the elephant. It was five feet high and six feet long. Now, we learned early on that it was a good idea to get the director's input on big decisions (such as the construction of an elephant). So we asked her to examine the wooden skeleton of the elephant once it was completed. She looked at it and said, "That is not my elephant!!" and left us to ponder her words.

We were somewhat shocked and at a loss. When the set coordinator tracked her down to get further input on what she meant, she said that it was about a third of the size that she needed. We proceeded to destroy our original attempt and rebuild the elephant. The final elephant was eight feet tall and approximately ten feet long. (Obviously it was stored in the auditorium where it stayed until the end of the show when it was dismantled). When someone sat on top, they were about eleven feet above the audience. You should have seen the look on the face of the boy who had to ride this pachyderm! At first he was terrified and then he worked his way down to unsettled. And did I mention that the elephant had to be able to move around the audience? The director's vision was that the elephant would start in the back of the auditorium, ride down one of the aisles up onto the stage, proceed across the stage, and then to the back of the auditorium down one of the aisles. The motoring power was supplied by two adults that were inside the elephant and the entire elephant rode on wheels. Now, I have to remind you of the size of the elephant, the fact that the stage was extended out into the audience (so space was limited), and the apprehension of the actor riding on its back. It sounds like a recipe for disaster! Well, it gets more interesting. The two fathers who were "driving" the elephant had no visibility at all, except for their feet and the four wheels that this colossal structure rode on. I was one of the lucky volunteers. I clearly remember shuffling along and looking for the corners of the stage so we wouldn't tip the elephant and send its rider off into the audience. It was simply unnerving. I am happy to report that no one died ...

Danielle and I in front of the "Elephant"

<u>And Let's Not Forget the Ship</u>

One of my other favorite set pieces was the ship. The director's instructions were that the ship had to be able to literally "sail" across the stage while accommodating four actors. Now, most set pieces were constructed with one-inch-by-two-inch lumber covered in sheets of styrofoam – not exactly the most structurally sound materials in the world! The ship was also to have masts that extended up to the ceiling which was about fifteen feet high. The set piece was needed for only one scene, so it had to be stored in the wings of the stage when not in use. While the set coordinator explained these parameters, I was just trying to process the information and get comfortable with the fact of whether it could be done. That's when he delivered the last piece of information: The ship had to be able to break in half and sink while on stage. I spent the rest of the afternoon crying…

Who could forget all of the glitter? Apparently glitter is the mainstay in the world of theater. Almost all of the set pieces were covered in a liberal coating of glitter. We were constantly being instructed to add more glitter. We were buying it by the buckets. We were using it by the buckets. We were going home covered in glitter. Years later, after my last show I was still finding glitter in my car!

Ryan and I with Danielle on Opening Night

I soon learned that my responsibilities did not end with constructing the set pieces. We were also expected to be the set crew during the play itself. Therefore, the couple of weekends before the play would be totally dedicated to putting the stage together and making sure everything worked properly. Then there was figuring out the set crew choreography of changing scenes. Unfortunately, we would sometimes be figuring things out on the opening night of the play.

Did you say Elevator?

During the weeks immediately preceding the play itself, there was the moment of discovery associated with the trap doors. You may have to read this twice, because the story is just too hard to believe. You see, several of the elevated stage sections had trap doors in them. The idea was that the actors could gain access to the stage by the trap door in the floor instead of just walking out from the wings. The trap doors themselves had to be solidly built because they had to accommodate the weight of children running over them when closed and had to simultaneously be easy to open for quick access.

During a rehearsal, I clearly recall the time when I was manning one of these trap doors. I was waiting for my cue to open it, allow the young actor to run up a small ladder and then to shut it quickly and secure the door. While waiting for my cue, this young man turned, looked at me, and asked, "Where's the elevator?" I told him that I was not aware of this detail and sent him scurrying up the ladder and out the trap door. Now this was a week or two before the play was to open, and up to that point, I had heard of no talk regarding an elevator. Being an engineer I know that elevators are rather complex devices, so I rationalized that this was misinformation. The young man obviously did not know what he was talking about! Later that afternoon I was talking to the set coordinator and laughed while I told him of my conversation regarding an "elevator." It was then that he showed me the crude sketch he had of the elevators he was going to construct later that afternoon. It was then that I knew that the huge expectations of the director had rubbed off onto him!

So the next thing I know, I am learning how to use this "elevator." Basically, it was a small platform that went up and down using a pulley system and was guided along by two rails. It had to be operated by two adults since there were pulleys on either side of the platform. We had to practice this operation many times since the two sides had to go up together or the platform would bind up or tip enough to cause the person riding on the platform to fall off. So here's the process to send someone up on the elevator: First, you had to unsecure the platform in the elevated section and drop it to the floor. Second, the actor had to stand on the platform. Then the two adults had to pull the wires simultaneously so the platform would rise and the actor would appear up on stage. Then the platform was secured in the up position. To make things a little more complicated, "smoke" from a fire extinguisher was shot up through the opening while the actor was coming up. We had four people working together in a space of about four feet by ten feet. Being in such tight quarters, we got to know each other quite well. It is my opinion that we were lucky not to have any incidents while using such a dubious device.

Well, we did have one minor incident. Everything appeared to be going along well. We had just finished sending this young man up on the elevator and had secured the platform in the up position. I was giving the other adult high fives when another member of the set crew came up to us in a panic and said we had to lower the platform immediately. She said the young man up on stage was apparently trapped. It turned out that we had pinched the young man's large elf-like shoes between the platform and the stage. He was essentially nailed down. He was heroically delivering his lines while unable to move. We quickly unsecured the platform and set him free.

Amazing in Many Ways

I will never forget the one show when they asked that all of the set crew wear costumes. Now we were supposed to be unseen, but there were moments where we might be spotted by the audience. I agreed to this condition without fully understanding what we were being asked to do. It turns out we were to wear black shirts and then tie some black cloth around us to make a pair of pants. Now just picture this in your head. Do you see it? Yes, it looked like we were wearing diapers!

It was a great group of guys to work with during my years on the set crew. The adverse conditions we worked under created true camaraderie. We would weather the storm together and we always succeeded. I will always look back upon the entire experience with awe and wonder.

Chapter 18

Morons Beware (of them)

Sir Charles Litton:

"He's either reloading or out of ammunition."

Inspector Clouseau:

"He's out of his mind. That's what he's out of."

From the movie "The Return of the Pink Panther"

Encountering a Bully

I was turning left onto northbound York Road from the Hereford Library access. Now before I go any further, you need to understand that downtown Hereford is very small and defined by one traffic light. There is a house on one corner and very small shopping plazas on the other two. My daughter and I had just stopped by the local snowball stand by the library where she had gotten an egg custard with marshmallow. After she consumed her snowball, we got into the car to go back home. I had waited for several cars to go by and it was clear to the left and right. I started to make the left turn. It was then that I saw the oncoming driver coming from the right but judged that I had enough time to safely make the left turn. When I realized that he was going at a faster rate of speed than I typically experienced in downtown Hereford, I had no choice but to speed up on the execution of the turn. After making the turn, I glanced into my rearview mirror and he was so close that I could not see his front bumper. He apparently did not want to use his brakes. He then proceeded to give me the middle finger and hand-signaled me to pull over – (I assume that he wanted to pass me or give me a piece of his mind). I hand-signaled for him to slow down since I thought he was driving way too aggressively for this stretch of road.

He proceeded to continue tailgating me for over two miles to the entrance of my community. I never saw his front bumper once and he kept hand-signaling for me to pull over. I could clearly see in my rearview mirror that he was obviously shouting.

When we arrived at the entrance of our community, I began turning right. It was then that he pulled right alongside me and called me an ___hole. I proceeded into the community and decided to slow down so I could get his license plate number. The way he was driving he could very well kill someone. He proved me right by slamming on his brakes and swerving onto the shoulder. He then put his car into reverse. I was intrigued to see what he had to say and thought that this would be a good opportunity to show my 13-year-old daughter how to constructively handle a bullying situation.

He stopped his car and proceeded to verbally assault me. I told him that he should not drive when he was so angry. He didn't take kindly to my comment. The last thing I recall him saying was that if I stepped out my car he would kick my butt. He and I then proceeded to drive off in our separate ways. I sure hope he didn't kill someone.

Chapter 19

Here Comes the Substitute

Becoming One of Them

We can all remember being in high school and having the joy of a substitute teacher. We knew nothing worthwhile was going to get done that day and we would try to get away with everything and anything. Once there was a substitute, the rumors would circulate throughout the school with the speed of a brushfire and everyone would anticipate that class ... the class where anything could happen.

I am not sure why, but I decided to become a substitute teacher. I take that back. I ***can*** actually remember ***exactly*** why I decided to start. It began before I became a stay-at-home dad. As a civil engineer, I used to love to teach schoolchildren about what a civil engineer does and to try to get them excited about the vocation. There were visits to my kids' daycare programs where we essentially got down on our hands and knees and built with building blocks. We laid out cities so we could destroy them. (What is it with kids and this Godzilla mentality)?!?!

Then there were also career days at the local elementary schools. I had a demonstration where I would build a bridge several different ways with the same materials, but each successive bridge would be stronger than the last. I would then go on to describe a typical workday, some of the benefits and challenges of being a civil engineer, and what skills the kids should have if they were interested in becoming an engineer. My outreach to the middle schools and high schools was primarily through a formal program. This program was actively recruiting the best and brightest students to get involved with engineering. My presentations were more specific for these students. I actually developed a sample transportation planning project which included an aerial photograph with a lot of natural and man-made features such as wetlands, forests, farms, communities, hazardous waste sites, and streams to demonstrate things we had to deal with when considering the placement of a new road. The students could draw concepts right onto the map, which would then be discussed and refined. It was very interesting to observe their thought processes and to discuss the various alternatives. I also made similar presentations to the Boy Scouts and Girls Scouts. I really enjoyed working with the students and the scouts, realizing I had the potential of making a small impact on their lives. In addition, I had numerous adults come up to me and tell me I should consider teaching as a vocation. Hence, the seed was planted.

Here We Go!

Fast forward several years to my being at home after "retiring." I decided to sample what it would be like to be a teacher by becoming a substitute. There were volumes of paperwork to fill out and, of course, the fingerprinting and background check. You will be thrilled to know that everything came back clear. I was given the go-ahead to substitute.

My first assignment was a real eye-opener. I was asked to substitute for a kindergarten class. I was oblivious and had no idea what to expect. I called the elementary school the day I got the kindergarten assignment to ask what I should wear and what was the earliest time I could report. My mind was racing a hundred miles an hour as I tried to anticipate what was in store for me. I had more questions than answers when I arrived.

Slowly Getting Overwhelmed

Everyone on the staff was very nice and kept telling me that if I needed anything to just let them know. I arrived about a half hour before the students. The kindergarten teacher had left instructions on what to do. The instructions were ***seven*** pages long and supplemented with yellow sticky notes and things written in the margins! These instructions were for less than three hours of instruction and were ***very*** detailed. It was not a simple matter of just reading them but understanding what the logistics were. For instance, the instructions told me that the students would put their star folders in the blue crate. Well after reading this instruction, I looked around for the blue crate so I would be better equipped to provide guidance. Every instruction pretty much required me to find a book or an audio visual and I was slowly being overwhelmed as I determined that I could not get through all of the instructions prior to the students' arrival. I was almost finished page three when they arrived.

Thank goodness there was a parent helper that day named Suzy. She was invaluable since she really knew how things worked in the classroom. The kindergarteners were quick to tell me how I was "doing it wrong" and I had to gently remind them that this is the way that Mr. Jim was going to do it! I was amazed at how busy the classroom was. There were teachers and specialists popping in throughout the morning taking various students to various places. My head was spinning but I plowed forward.

Some Thrills ... and Chaos

One of the highlights for me was when I got to read the book *Big Pumpkin*. It is truly magical when you read to children of any age. No matter how crazy things are around you, the children always seem to calm down when you read to them. I always try to make it fun by changing my voice for various characters or getting them involved in the story. I truly enjoy reading to children.

One of the more challenging moments in the day was during the Centers activity. Basically during this activity, all of the children go to stations throughout the room and do different activities. The kids know what to do so even though there is a lot, and I mean ***a lot,*** of stuff going on, it is pretty organized. The challenge is trying to monitor all that is going on. So there I was running to and fro trying to make sure everyone was okay. Ms. Suzy had just stepped out to take some of the kids to the book fair so I was all by myself. And that is when I heard the cry, "Mr. Jim, Mr. Jim!! I need you to come over here quick!" I rushed over to the painting center to find that one of the buckets of paint had dropped to the floor and essentially exploded. There was paint everywhere including all over Johnny! Once the kids knew that there was an incident, they all wanted to see what happened. So now there is paint all over the floor, paint all over Johnny, and kids all converging on the scene. The irony was that my parent helper was gone and there was no way I could get any of the help that had been so generously offered previously. I had to work my way through this and quickly. We were on a tight schedule! Fortunately, we prevailed.

At the very end of the day, the kids were all dressed in their winter jackets and waiting for the buses. They were getting a bit antsy, so Ms. Suzy recommended that we play a game like Simon Says. Well I am good at leading games but not so good at knowing when to bend the rules. Let me elaborate. I started the game and made it relatively simple since I wanted the children to have a good time and we had several minutes to kill before the buses arrived. So I started off and everyone was doing well. Then I switched it up and, of course, several kids were eliminated. When they were eliminated, they were instructed to sit down. Everyone was having fun until I told one boy - let's call him Carl - to sit down since he had touched his ears which Simon had not instructed him to do. That's when he crumpled to the floor and started to profess that he was an idiot and how could he be so stupid? Well, I had a choice to make: I could either attend to his specific need thereby abandoning the rest of the class, or I could proceed with the game and ignore him while he sobbed on the floor. It was then that I came up with a new and brilliant idea. I looked at Ms. Suzy and asked her to take care of him. I mean, it was her idea to play this game so she should have to deal with the consequences!

<u>Going Back for More</u>

I survived that first day and went on to substitute for elementary, middle, and high school classes. I substituted for a wide variety of subjects including English, Math, Science, Social Studies, Music, Physical Education, Business, and Library Science. I would report to different schools, have different students and faculty to interact with, and always have the issue of finding where the faculty bathrooms were located. Every day was an adventure and the real irony is that my personality is one that does not enjoy change. I prefer knowing what I am doing on a daily basis and here I was getting called at 5:30 in the morning to tell me where my services were needed. You know that I really have to believe in the value of teaching to put myself in a situation that goes against my natural grain.

I tried to substitute in the schools close to my home since it shortened my day and allowed me to make enough money to cover my gas costs (ha ha). Of course this meant that there was a chance that I would be substituting in one of my children's schools or even worse ... in one of their classes. This did not bother Ryan, but Danielle was mortified at the thought of me being her teacher. Whenever I got an assignment, she would immediately want to know for which school. If the school was hers, then she would want to know for whom I was substituting. One day I was substituting in her school, but it was not one of her teachers. Once I arrived at the school they told me that things had changed and I was now substituting for someone else. Danielle was very surprised to see me later that day. We were able to muddle through that situation, just like I had been able to muddle through all of the ones before!

Chapter 20

Wanna Buy Some Rocks?

Good is All Around Us

There is a lot of good in the world. I believe you can find it in others and almost everything that is going on around us. Whether it is a stranger just saying "hi" or a beautiful sunset, there is good around almost every corner. You just have to be open to it. This philosophy is one of my core beliefs. I have to say that I don't base this philosophy on what I see on television or read in the newspaper. What I do base it on are the events in my life ...

Coping with a Tragic Time

It was a sad time in our lives. Michele's father had just passed away after a heroic battle with cancer. The family was in shock as the patriarch of the family was no longer there. We were all trying to cope with the loss, pick up the pieces, and move on with our lives. We stopped over to visit Michele's mom to talk about many of the details that need to be tended to after someone passes away. The house was full of people young and old alike.

I felt like a third wheel as Michele was handling things on her own as she usually does. The kids were bored out of their minds since no one was paying attention to them and there was nothing for them to do. Jessica, our nephew's wife, had Sadie who was about seven and Julian who was about three with her. When I asked her what I could do with them she suggested that we go sell some rocks. I was somewhat perplexed by her response. She explained to me that the kids had come up with the idea earlier in the spring and were excited to give their new business a shot.

A Business Venture

I went up to Sadie and Julian and asked them about these rocks they were looking to sell. They took me by the hand and led me to a five-gallon plastic bucket. There in the bottom were several non-descript rocks. I asked them how they thought we should sell the rocks. They suggested that we go door-to-door throughout the neighborhood. The houses in the community are not very close together, and it was the middle of the day on a weekday so I knew most people were going to be at work. However, I wanted to encourage their independent approach so I agreed.

The first obstacle that arose was dragging the bucket of rocks around. The kids kindly asked if I would carry the bucket of rocks and I politely said "no." It was my opinion that they were strong enough to carry the bucket of rocks and I wanted them to feel the sense of accomplishment, (although I was beginning to have doubts after going to our first house and no one was home).

After lugging the bucket of rocks to the second house and finding no one there, I made a suggestion: Why don't we set up a couple of chairs at the end of the driveway and create a sign so people driving by could stop and buy the rocks? The kids thought about it and agreed. Now I wasn't really sure this was going to work. The community is rather small and most people were at work, but it was better than hauling that bucket of rocks around. We got set up and before long a neighbor drove by. They stopped and I thought to myself that maybe there could be some rewards here for these two young entrepreneurs. The neighbors offered their condolences to the family but said they were not interested in buying any rocks. I have to say I wasn't very surprised, but it would have been nice if they had bought one.

A Moment of True Impact

About twenty minutes or so went by without a single car driving by. This is what I thought would happen, but you could see that the kids were excited about the prospect of making a sale, especially with the close call with the neighbor. Off in the distance I saw the mail delivery truck approaching. My hopes for a sale were not high as I considered the nature of this person's job. I thought that there was no way he or she would slow down, let alone purchase a rock. I was wrong. She stopped her mail truck and asked the kids what they were doing. They spent a couple of minutes describing how they had found the rocks, put them in the bucket, and were selling them. The mail lady listened intently and showed genuine interest. I was very impressed. I mean the kids were just selling rocks! It was then that she brought out her small change purse. The kids explained how the rocks were one dollar each. I was amazed that she was buying a rock. You can imagine my shock when she said she wanted two! The kids took her money and let her select two of the rocks. As she drove away, the kids thanked her and I sat there in amazement. She did not have to stop. She did not have to listen to the kids. She did not have to buy any of their rocks. But she did and her act of kindness changed me.

Chapter 21

The Not-So-Mini Minivan

Taking the Plunge

I own a minivan. If you had asked me twenty years ago if I would ever own one I probably would have laughed in your face. Look who's laughing now ...

Michele and I decided to get a minivan in the fall of 2001. Ryan had just turned ten and Danielle was five. We needed to keep the kids entertained on our long vacation trips or visits to family and friends who lived in far-away places. Up to that point in time we had sometimes borrowed Michele's parents' conversion van. We could see how advantageous the concept of owning a van was. We finally came to the realization that we needed to purchase a minivan and it would have to come with the built in VCR player, (of course). Essentially we would have a movie theater on wheels. It turned out to be an extraordinary idea.

The minivan handled like a car but provided plenty of room and allowed us to keep the kids occupied on the longer trips. We watched many of the animated classics like *Lion King, Little Mermaid,* and *The Incredibles.* Of course there were the classics like *The Little Princess, October Sky,* and *Remember the Titans.* Comedies were also very popular and included *Galaxy Quest, Christmas Vacation,* or any one of the *Pink*

Panther movies featuring Peter Sellers. Everything went smoothly, but we knew that there had to be a bump or two along the way.

A Tough Encounter

The "bump" came when the minivan was full of kids and we were showing them a movie. One of the kids sitting way in the back abruptly had to release the contents of his stomach. The release was so quick that there was no warning and, before I knew what was going on, it was over. We pulled over and once he was out of the car and got some fresh air, he was fine. The van, on the other hand, was not fine. I don't know if you have been caught in this predicament, but it is not pleasant. I did the best I could cleaning up the mess, but it was impossible to remove all of the vomit which was embedded in the carpeting and the car seat and seemed to be everywhere. I covered the seat with a trash bag. The wretched odor remained and I was thankful that the smell did not make anyone else get sick. I made the kid who had thrown up move up to the front passenger seat where he was less likely to get sick again. Since I had no extra seats, I had to make one of the other kids sit in the foul-smelling seat.

There's a Lesson in There

The rest of the trip was incident-free, but I learned a valuable lesson that day. Many people get motion sickness while riding in a car. I believe that they get sick because their mind knows that the body is sitting down in the car, but the eyes are witnessing movement in the scenery that is whizzing past the vehicle. This creates a mental paradox and a person can begin to feel queasy. The equation gets more complicated when you introduce the movie. Now the mind knows that the body is stationary, but the eyes are witnessing movement on the screen and simultaneously seeing a different kind of movement in their peripheral vision of the countryside flying by. My theory is substantiated when you consider that the young man did not get sick until the movie was stopped. I think this drastic change in his visual/motion experience caused him to feel sick. After that incident, I did not show movies to any kids other than my own. That way if I am cleaning up vomit, at least it is my own family's vomit.

Some Parting Observations

The minivan is an extremely versatile vehicle. When all of the seats are in place, it acts like a very nice bus. The salesman told me it accommodates seven people and there are seven seat belts. However, the only way the minivan will accommodate seven people is if the riders have what I like to call "tiny hinies." When you remove all of the seats, it becomes a parcel van, which I have filled from the floor to the roof with supplies for my two businesses or a load of stuff to sell at a local yard sale. I can pop out the last two seats and create a large cargo area for luggage while keeping four comfortable seats for the passengers. I can remove the two passenger side seats so I can accommodate some lumber that I purchased at the local hardware store. The bottom line is that I love my minivan and I would consider buying another one when this one stops working. By the way, don't forget vomit bags attached to the back of each seat. They can come in handy!!

Chapter 22

Philmont

A Trip of a Lifetime Begins

A trip to Philmont is one of the opportunities that the older Boy Scouts have. Philmont is a High Adventure Scout Reservation located in the Sangre de Cristo (Blood of Christ) range of the Rocky Mountains in New Mexico. It is 137,493 acres (215 square miles) of rough terrain with an elevation ranging from 6,500 to 12,441 feet. There are deer, cougar, coyotes, elk, antelope, wild turkeys, bears, beavers, buffalo, and many other wild animals roaming throughout the hills and canyons. It is truly a magical place. What makes it a high adventure experience is that you carry everything you need on your back, and head out into the wilderness where you learn how to survive as a group. The gear that you carry includes your tent, clothing, food, essential equipment, and water. It is surprising to learn that the water is, by far, the heaviest thing you have to carry. They say you need up to one gallon per day to stay hydrated and this is eight pounds of your total backpack weight.

The typical plan for a trip out to Philmont is that you fly out to Denver, Colorado and spend a couple of days traveling to Cimarron, New Mexico. Then you spend a day in base camp getting acclimated to the higher elevation, which is 6,000 feet above sea level. Finally, you get to backpack all throughout the reservation based on the itinerary you picked beforehand. Your itinerary can include backpacking from two to twelve miles per day and participating in various activities once you get to your camp for that day. Activities include burro racing, rock climbing, horseback riding, gold panning, mountain biking, .30/06 rifle shooting, tomahawk throwing, wood pole climbing, interpretive history lessons, and chuck wagon dinners. You are in the reservation for a total of twelve days. Sadly, you must return home. These are excerpts from the journal that I kept during this incredible trip. I entered them in at the end of each day:

Day 1 – Tradition holds as Ryan got sick this morning as we got off the plane in Denver. His stomach has always been a little queasy. I guess I shouldn't have fed him one of those big greasy egg and sausage sandwiches for breakfast. Our crew consisted of eight scouts and four adult leaders from our troop. We were picked up from the airport by a 56-passenger bus. We had more room than we knew what to do with! We were able to visit some of the sights along the way to Philmont. Our first stop was the Garden of Gods. The rock formations popped up right out of the ground and were a beautiful reddish-brown color. It kind of reminded me of a kid's room after he has played with blocks and forgot to put them away. We were hiking along the trails which were intertwined between all of these incredible rock formations. The formations were huge, but I didn't realize how big they were until I saw rock climbers on them. It was a bit surreal as I watched this person, who appeared to be the size of an ant, climbing this rock that looked like a 200-foot high finger sticking straight up out of the earth. I am not a big rock climber myself, but I find it interesting to watch. That night we stayed at the Koshare Indian Museum. They had created a meeting room designed like the ones built by early Indians of the area. The roof contained six hundred logs and only seven nails. It was very impressive.

Day 2 – The Koshares were very hospitable. I am pretty sure I stayed at this same location when I came here as a Boy Scout over thirty years ago. (I forgot to mention that I went to Philmont as a gift from my mom and dad for earning the rank of Eagle Scout). Anyway, we finally arrived at base camp, which was located at the base of the mountain called "The Tooth of Time." It gets its name from the fact that it looks like a solitary tooth and has been used as a notable landmark for hundreds of years. We stayed in big canvas tents similar to the ones found at most summer camps. We set up for our overnight stay and then met our trail guide named Alex who liked to go by the name of "Qwaar." If you think that sounded odd, then you would also have to take my word for it that his nickname was similar to his personality. It was Qwaar's job to tag along with our crew for the first day or so to make sure that we knew what we were doing.

Joe, one of the other adults in our crew, as well as one of my best friends, and I went in search of some adventure when we determined we had some time to kill. (It turned out that we sat around a lot waiting for lunch, gear, paperwork, etc.). Joe, who owns his own towing company and loves tow trucks, learned that the Philmont Scout Reservation has its own tow trucks. Well this became our mission as we went off to find one of these tow trucks. After walking for a little while, we were picked up by a passing car. They gladly took us to the motor pool where we found the tow truck. We took plenty of pictures and then found ourselves racing back to the lodge. Walking several miles back to camp definitely did not go as quickly as the drive! Joe stated that he liked it better in the shade. We attended a church service that was quite nice. A seminarian helped out with the Mass and did an excellent job. For me, this was the perfect way to begin our high adventure experience.

Day 3 – Finally, our adventure began as we started hiking today! It rained throughout the night, but we stayed dry in our nice big tents. Before hitting the trail, we took a nice cold shower which was not only exhilarating, but it dawned on me that this was probably the closest thing to a modern convenience that we would experience for the next eleven days. I weighed my fully loaded backpack and it was forty pounds. I recalled that the rule of thumb was that it should weigh from twenty-five to thirty percent of my body weight. I sat down to do the computation. Let's see ... my weight is ... therefore, I should be able to carry about ... I figured out that I would be fine! We got on a bus which took us to the location where our hike was to begin. At first it was sunny, and then some ominous clouds began to develop. By the time we got there, it was a deluge. I mean the skies just opened up and it was torrential! Fortunately, we were all prepared and therefore, had the appropriate rain gear. The only catch was that the rain gear was in the back of the bus with our packs and we were seated up front. So we arrived at our destination, climbed out of the bus, became immediately doused, unloaded the backpacks, and calmly put on our rain gear including our backpack covers in the hard pounding rain. No one in our crew complained. That was probably because we all knew that it does no good to complain. We understood that "rain is rain." There's nothing we could have done about it. All we could do was work with it. If there is one thing that Boy Scouts has taught me, it has been that a cheerful disposition goes a long way when facing adverse conditions.

This was a point in our journey where there was a funny story to tell. However before I tell it, I need to explain something. Philmont is very large. Philmont is very rustic and wild. There are no signs to tell you where to go. We had been provided a map and compass, and the trails are relatively well worn. With all of this being said, it is fair to say that it is very common for crews to get lost at one time or another during their journey. Getting lost is ***part*** of the journey ... So enough of that! Let's get back to our story. There we were standing in the pouring rain. One of the boys was studying the map. As the designated navigator, he knew it was his job to tell us which way to go. There was a trail in front of us. We had two options. We could either go left or right. The boy thought about it and told us to go to the right. We proceeded about a hundred feet and came to a barbed wire fence. We all thought that was odd, especially since we had been instructed that a barbed wire fence typically ran along the boundary of the reservation. We then put two and two together and well… you guessed it! The first several steps of our journey had been taken in the wrong direction. (Looking back on this day, I am happy to report that that is the only time we got lost in the eleven days on the trail hiking approximately one hundred miles. I was very proud of the boys for their orienteering skills).

We hiked only two miles today to the un-staffed Anasazi site. Once again it was a test to see how well prepared we were. The two miles were rather arduous since the rain turned the trail into slick mud. It was very difficult to navigate without slipping and falling. We saw a fossilized footprint of a Tyrannosaurus Rex and finally made it to our campsite for the night. We then set up camp.

Dehydrated food will be the primary type of food that we eat while out on the trail. Dinner was the wonderful dehydrated meal of rice and refried beans. It was a good meal in that it really stuck to our ribs. However, the after-effect was rather disgusting but somewhat amusing. We all had tremendous gas and spent the rest of the night farting. Ryan had a tremendous fart that cleared everyone out of the fire ring area. He got a reputation tonight that was well-deserved. I am confident that he will keep it going throughout the entire time we are on the trail.

Today, we learned a lot of neat camping tips to help us on our journey. One of the concerns of being in Philmont is the bears. We were informed that the bears like campers since we are a source of food. As a result, we were also educated that each night we would have to remove all of our gear that had any type of smell. We were instructed that any gear that had smell needed to be placed in a "bear bag" each night. This included band aids, duct tape, food (obviously), cooking gear, soap, sunscreen, toothbrushes, toothpaste, bug repellent, and even film. A bear bag is a large bag filled with all of the crew's "smellables" and then hoisted up on ropes that are stretched between two trees. When it is finally in place, the bag is about twenty feet up in the air. The whole set-up process took about thirty to forty-five minutes every evening. We had to take this bear situation very seriously. So there I was on our first night after being out on the trail. I recall making a conscious decision that I was going to take care of myself while in Philmont. It was something that I usually regarded as an option on most previous camping trips. So I started to brush my teeth before going to bed. There I was brushing just outside of our small two-man tent. It dawned on me that I did not want to spit the toothpaste concoction that was in my mouth right by our tent. I was pretty sure that this would attract the bears. So I had a dilemma. I was not sure what to do. Well, sometime during all of our preparing, I had heard that an option was to swallow the toothpaste. So that is what I did. It wasn't that bad, but I wouldn't do it voluntarily!

Day 4 - We were up by 5:45 a.m. and hitting the trail by 7:00 a.m. This was the way it would be most days, which was fine with me since we typically went to bed when the sun went down anyway. Each day you get up you have to pack up all that is in the tent, bring down the bear bags, get gear out of bear bags, take down the tent and pack it up, load up on water, and grab a quick bite. We hiked to a place called Indian Writing. There we met some of the Philmont staff. Most of the staff was funny as well as witty. The staff at Indian Writing was no exception. We got to see a number of petroglyphs, which are rock drawings by the native Indians. And we saw some archeological digs, which were also from Indians that were once settled in the area. I began to understand why they named this place as they did.

We hiked four miles today. We saw giant chipmunks as well as some of the largest beetles I had ever seen. It was like the animals were all on steroids! We got to our camp called Cottonwood at 12:30 p.m. so we had some time to kill. Since there were no televisions, game systems, cell phones, or texting opportunities, we found ourselves occupying our time in different ways. Alternative activities included the washing of clothes, taking naps, playing hacky sack, making miniature forts in the dirt, playing cards, talking, or taking a bucket bath. We also partook in a reflection exercise. We all went to isolated spots around our camp just to sit still, listen carefully, and just reflect on where we were and what we were doing. It was a very powerful experience as we sat and absorbed the magnificent countryside that surrounded us.

The vegetation is very unique in Philmont. One of my favorite trees was the Ponderosa Pine. These trees were not only beautiful, but they smelled wonderful. Want to guess what they smelled like? Ok you can stop guessing. They smelled like a combination of vanilla and butterscotch. These are two of my favorite flavors, so I found myself going up regularly and smelling them. Most people would look at that behavior as being odd and a bit crazy. However, everyone in our crew seemed to understand and I occasionally found them smelling the trees as well.

The food continued to be good. The boys ate it all. In fact, they had to eat it all in order to not attract any bears. After everyone has eaten, one boy is selected to be the "human sump." It was his job to scrape all food out of the cooking pans and eat it. Sometimes licking the pan was required. This minimized the amount we had to throw away and allowed the boys to maintain their body weight while burning thousands of extra calories a day.

Cooking the food was a bit "scary" since we used white gas stoves. The advantage to these stoves is that they are portable and the gas is a liquid and can be refilled whenever an opportunity comes up. The disadvantage is the stove itself. The stove needs to be pre-heated to build up pressure in the gas tank. The way you pre-heat the stove is to dump some gas on it and then light the stove on fire. It seemed a bit crazy and I have to admit it was very intimidating!

I was pretty sure that if Ryan kept farting he would be kicked out of the group. Unfortunately, even when he was not the culprit, he was the one blamed! It almost seemed like a conspiracy. The dehydrated food we ate was very good. The food that we ate was the kind that stuck with us but made us a bit gassy. For instance, tonight's meal was red rice on a tortilla shell. It was awesome but kept Ryan's "gun loaded."

Day 5 - We hit the trail again early in the morning to get to Ponil. It was our first challenging day since we were traveling about eight miles. The first 2.87 miles were done in an hour. We knew this because our GPS unit told us all kinds of stuff like elevation, where we were, how far we had traveled, etc. We finished the eight miles in four and a half hours. Along the way we saw many wonderful, as well as intriguing, things along the trail. There were beautiful black and yellow birds, deer, elk, black and orange birds, rock erosion that looked like a whale, big squirrels, and, of course, all kinds of scat (poop from various animals). For lunch there was the wonderful treat of dehydrated pineapples. I really like dehydrated pineapples. They are sweet and chewy. I wondered how I could get more …

I forgot to mention that we had been washing our clothes by hand and when we woke up in the morning, they were still a bit wet. Instead of packing the wet clothes into our packs, soaking everything else in our packs and creating a moldy situation, we used safety pins and pinned our laundry onto our packs so they could dry while we hiked. It was quite funny to see everyone hiking along with underwear hanging from their packs!

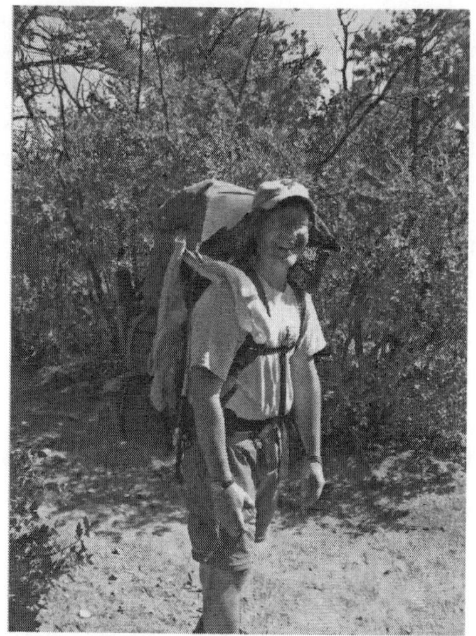

The economical way to dry your underwear!

We climbed to the top of Hart Peak which has an elevation of 7,975 feet. There was a wonderful view from the top. You could see for probably a hundred miles in each direction. We were very fortunate in that the weather had been phenomenal. It had been in the low 80's with occasional winds. The lack of humidity allowed us to take in these spectacular views and take some nice photographs.

Andrew is our crew leader. He was elected by the boys before we left for the trip. He is doing a good job. He isn't afraid to make decisions, stand by the decisions he makes, and he admits when his decisions could have been better.

These are all the traits that the adults try to instill into all of our boy leaders.

When we arrived at Ponil, we got oriented by the staff. This was where we heard the infamous "hummingbird" story. It went something like this ... The staff sets up hummingbird feeders at each of the headquarter buildings and the hummingbirds love it! It is kind of surreal for hikers getting closer to camp since you see and hear more hummingbirds the closer you get. It is like when you approach an airport. Anyway, the story was that one scout was hit in the eye by a flying hummingbird. For any of you who may not know what a hummingbird looks like, imagine a small bird about the size of your thumb with wings that flap so fast that you cannot see them and it has a needle-like straw for a beak. The thought of one stuck in your eye made me feel all squeamish inside. Unfortunately, the story got worse. They had to kill the hummingbird while it was in the scout's eye to prevent it from thrashing around and causing more damage. "How do you kill a hummingbird?" you may wonder. Well in order to kill the cuddly creature, one has to squeeze the life out of it. Once the hummingbird was dead, they had to transport the scout to a medical facility. I cannot even begin to imagine what it must have been like to travel with a dead hummingbird hanging out of your eye. That had to be one of the longest trips in the history of man!

We set up our camp and then participated in some of the activities there. Many of us got our hats and boots branded with the Philmont brand. The boys learned how to use the lasso and got to practice on the "cows." Actually the "cows" were sawhorses with heads. It was funny to watch the boys try to master this skill. We also completed our service project. We picked rocks out of the surrounding countryside, brought them down to the sledging area, and crushed them with sledge hammers. It was just the way I had pictured chain gang work by prisoners. The only thing missing was a prison guard with a shotgun! That night there was a chuck wagon dinner. This was the only location on the trail where others would be feeding us. (Actually I state that loosely, since we had to provide adults from our crew to help prepare the meal).

The sky that night was simply amazing. Without any "light pollution," it seemed like you could see forever. The Milky Way was plainly visible, which is something we cannot see at home. In addition, we could see satellites racing across the sky. (No, that is ***not*** a misprint). Viewing the night sky helped me to keep things in perspective.

Day 6 – Surprise! Surprise! The adults got up at 5:00 a.m. to cook breakfast for everyone. We started hiking at 8:45 a.m. Today was a bit unique since the trails were cut out of steep hill faces. Parts of the trail were actually missing due to erosion. We would have to run across these missing portions of the trail and hope we didn't lose our forward momentum. Otherwise we would have slipped and then fell down the downhill side. It was a bit unnerving because you could not see the bottom! We safely arrived in the Pueblo Ruins by noon. I realized that each day was bringing us closer to Baldy Mountain, the highest elevation in the reservation.

Our crew had begun a "food trading" program. As I mentioned before, I enjoyed the dehydrated pineapple. It was very delectable and energized me as well. Some of the other boys in our crew loved the beef jerky (which I find a bit putrid), so a trade was made. It was a win-win situation as I continued to consume huge amounts of dehydrated pineapple.

At Pueblo Ruins we were exposed to various logging activities. The first one was pole climbing just like what the utility guys do. A leather strap was put around us as well as the thirty-foot-high pole; then our boots were fitted with spikes; then we donned a pair of gloves, and at last we climbed the pole using the proper technique. Once we got to the top, we were supposed to kiss the pulley associated with the safety line. I am not a big pole climber, so I was definitely outside of my comfort zone on this exercise. Most of the boys made it to the top in about two minutes. I made is in just under five minutes. I didn't post a good time, but I was successful! By the way, I had never kissed such a beautiful pulley!

Then it was off to a game of Logger Ball. This is a game developed by the staff. It was just like baseball with one exception … there were no rules! The boys had a great time until the game ended when a strange boy got hold of the ball and went off running into the wilderness with it. We still haven't seen him ...

That evening there was a campfire put on by the staff. It was the first real campfire since being at Philmont. Campfires were allowed (there had been no restrictions while we had been here), but building them is a bit laborious. You see, after you have burned your fire, you have to make sure it is completely out (obviously), put it into a bag (what?!?), haul it a certain distance from your campsite, carry it off the trail a certain distance (I think it was couple of hundred feet), and finally scatter the ashes. This seemed to be a bit much just to have a little warmth and glow from a fire. So we decided that if the staff was going to put on a fire program, we were going to attend. Obviously the campfire was held at night, but that created another situation. You see, it was recommended by Philmont that every other boy carry a flashlight in order to save on space and weight in our backpacks. On the surface this sounded like a good idea. However, when you had to hike at night, that idea didn't seem so good. So after the campfire, we began our hike back to our campsite. It was about a one-mile hike and it was dark - really dark. To make matters a little more challenging, it was raining as well. So we started back to camp in the rain and into pitch blackness. Everything was going well until we came across our first stream crossing. Now this was not a dry streambed. It was about twenty feet wide and about a foot deep. This was somewhat challenging when you consider that we only had a total of six small flashlights. We did make it across that stream crossing and the second one as well. By the time we got back to our campsite, we were exhausted and bit frazzled. It was time to hit the sack!

Day 7 – Today's hike to Miranda was short but intense. The lack of adequate sleep (we only got from six and a half to seven hours a night) and the strenuous activity were starting to wear us down a bit. Speaking of strenuous activity, the various treks offered by Philmont are all given a difficulty ranking. There is Challenging, Rugged, Strenuous and Super Strenuous. When we first began meeting back in the fall, we all agreed that we wanted to do the Strenuous since it seemed to fit the character of our group. We did not know it until we got to Philmont, but we got stuck with a Super Strenuous trek because the trek we had originally wanted had already filled up!

Another thing to note is that some of the other crews use horses to get around while others use burros to carry their equipment. The burros were a bit ornery. I recall one incident when I heard several things said about them including, "Burros are not worth it. They suck." Miranda was a very nice camp. There were beautiful wildflowers everywhere and a nice stand of birch trees. Mount Baldy was very close now and made a beautiful backdrop to the camp.

We had a camp orientation as we do in all of the staffed camps. A young man named Mike greeted us. He was dressed all in back woodsman garb, which included fur clothes, tomahawk and all, and he was telling us all we needed to know. I happened to notice that there was a rather large chipmunk hanging out in front of the staff headquarters building. Now when I say chipmunk, I was not sure that it was truly a chipmunk. All the animals we'd seen are massive and they look like they are on steroids! Anyway, this particular chipmunk got the attention of Mike and, (this is where it gets funny), without thinking he threw his tomahawk at the chipmunk. I was totally shocked and horrified. All I could think was this is a lose-lose situation. If he hit the chipmunk, we would get to witness the killing of one of God's creatures, live and in person. If he missed the chipmunk, then others could be in danger. Well, he missed the chipmunk (thank goodness) and the tomahawk went flying past the chipmunk, hit a rock, and ricocheted toward the front of the headquarters where several adults were hanging out on the front porch. The tomahawk's handle hit one of the adult's hands but he was okay (thank goodness). Looking back on the whole incident, it was obvious that Mike did not think before he acted. In fact, he looked as surprised as the rest of us when he threw the tomahawk.

We did some really cool activities at Miranda including throwing tomahawks (like Mike) and shooting black powder rifles. The throwing of tomahawks was made interesting by trying to hit a playing card posted on a large cut section of a felled tree. In the first four throws, I hit the playing card twice and got one axe to actually stick in the wood. Not bad. In shooting the black powder rifle, the first round was a fifty-charge and then the staff had a surprise for the adults and put in a one hundred-charge. What a kick! We were all allowed to place something downrange before the shooting began so we all went back to camp with a shot up hat or bandana.

As we looked to the Baldy Summit, we all wondered what tomorrow would have in store for us ...

Day 8 – This was the only camp where we didn't have to tear down the camp first thing in the morning because we were staying here for two days. The reason we were staying here for two days was that today was the day we were to summit Baldy Mountain. The hike was quite challenging from the very first step because every step was uphill. There were frequent breaks and there were times when it felt like we were getting nowhere. It kept getting steeper and steeper as we approached the summit. We would take ten to twenty steps and then stop for thirty seconds to catch our breath. Not only was the climb taxing our physical strength, but there was inadequate oxygen as well! We had risen about 3,500 feet in elevation in just one day.

After much effort, we finally reached the summit! The view was spectacular. It was like you could see forever. There were various mountains and mountain ranges everywhere you looked. There were valleys, farms, forests, lakes and you could see the weather as it occurred. Everything was on a grand scale. It took my breath away since it kind of put me in my place, and it was just amazingly beautiful.

We ate lunch in what had to be the most glorious setting imaginable. After lunch, we took a whole bunch of pictures. I think we all realized that this was something very special and it might be a while before we had another adventure like this again.

We proceeded down on the other side of the summit. The trip down was to be just as memorable as the trip up. It was a twenty-degree downgrade and it was all large rock that slid while I slid. It was not a hike for the faint-hearted. A storm was coming from the direction we were heading so we had to come down in a hurry. We got out of the really high elevations but not before the pea-sized hail started to come down. After we descended about a thousand feet, we came across a large snowfield and the boys went sledding on their packs. We then proceeded down for a while before we came to the French Henry Mining and Milling Company. Here the boys worked with the blacksmiths to build a "J" hook. They also panned for gold but had to stop early since we still had to hike to Baldy Town to pick up food and then hike back to Miranda where our camp awaited us. I clearly remember the quartermaster at Miranda giving our crew fresh fruit as a treat. It truly was a treat since it wasn't dehydrated like everything else we had been eating up to that point. It was a long day of hiking … about thirteen and a half hours encompassing twelve miles. This is what I would call "super strenuous," but it certainly was an incredible experience.

Day 9 - Up at 5:00 a.m. After taking down camp and eating a quick breakfast, we hit the trail and hiked several miles to Head of Dean where there was a COPE course. The purpose of a COPE course is to get a crew of boys to work together to accomplish various tasks while facing numerous obstacles. For instance, our crew had one obstacle where they all started on one side of a rather large "pit" and had to swing across one by one using a rope swing. The first challenge was to get the rope hanging in the middle of this twelve-foot-wide pit. If anyone fell into the pit, they had to start over. To make it even more challenging, they had to get a glass of water across the pit without spilling it. The highlight was watching the boys assist one boy who was struggling a bit. They cheered him on and helped him out. They strategized to solve the problem. They worked as a group and succeeded as a group.

After the COPE course, we hiked several more miles to the un-staffed Black Jack campsite. In a way the un-staffed camps were more fun. They were very quiet and peaceful. Black Jack was totally deserted except for us. It was also quite beautiful. After dinner, we decided to take ten minutes of solitude. Each scout and adult would pick a spot and sit in total silence. We would clear our minds and just reflect on what an incredible setting we were in. I ended up sitting there for more than ten minutes and took in the wonderful scene God put before me. There was a valley defined on one side by the ridge that we were sitting on top of and a string of mountains was across the way. The sky was simply breathtaking. There was a pale gray ceiling with voluminous cumulus clouds sprinkled about in the foreground. The entire scene was lit up by the sunset's rays breaking through the clouds and between the mountains. I literally cried because it was breathtakingly splendid.

Each night we would do "thorns and roses." This was an opportunity for each member of our crew to mention what they enjoyed about the day and ways that we could improve. This was followed by a devotional. This was where we would stand in a circle with our arms around each other and tell everyone what we were thankful for that day. I had to say that I was becoming less and less thankful for the dehydrated pineapples. They were starting to lose some of their appeal. I mean, how many dehydrated pineapple chunks can a person eat?

Day 10 – A gorgeous sky greeted us today. Everyone seemed to be in excellent spirits as there was a lot of joking around and singing. We played a game where we would name an old television show and then sing the theme song. Being on the trail was definitely more challenging for some than others. We had developed a cohesive unit and struck what I would like to call the "team" pace. Ten miles later, we ended up in the Harlan camp. The staff showed us how to make our own shotgun shells and then took us to the range to shoot some clay targets. I was lucky and hit five out of the six clay targets. The boys were allowed to shoot any of their personal gear (hats and bandanas) with the shotguns as a way to remember our trip. The staff seemed to enjoy shooting the boys' stuff as much as the boys did. The shotgun definitely had more kick than the black powder rifles.

That night the adults had the luxury of coffee on the front porch of the staff's cabin. There is nothing finer than a hot cup of coffee after a long day of adventure! While sipping our hot beverage, we were able to watch the boys participate in a burro race. The race consisted of having to guide your burro from the starting line up to a marker and then back. It sounds easier than it is. Our boys had the slowest and most ornery burro so they finished dead last. They did seem to have fun, though.

Day 11 - We were up at 5:00 a.m. but had to boil water for our breakfast which was not typical. As a result it took us a little longer to hit the trail. The trail today was a lot of up and down, so it was pretty taxing. We could see the Tooth of Time as well as base camp way off in the distance. It was apparent that the end was clearly in sight.

The camp of Cimmeroncito was quite beautiful. They actually had electricity! The boys took a hike to the food station to collect food for the last two days on the trail. A bear wandered through the camp while they were gone.

Once the boys got back, there was rock climbing and repelling. It was one of the boys' birthdays today so a lady staff member surprised him after he repelled down the cliff face with a great big hug. Everyone did very well and had a great time.

I would be remiss if I did not mention the bathroom facilities (or the lack thereof). Most of the time, you had to dig a hole to do your business and then bury it once you were done. However, there were latrines along the way. The fancy ones were called "Red Roof Inns" since they had a roof and kept you away from the rain while you tended to your business. The more interesting latrines were the ones found in the middle of nowhere sitting in the woods all by themselves but very visible from the trail. All I could think was how I would feel if I was taking care of business and someone came along the trail. I guess I would feel vulnerable, exposed, and embarrassed. It got even wackier when we came across a set of two toilets side by side with no walls or roof. I couldn't imagine who I would feel comfortable enough with to experience this situation. The roll of toilet paper and a shovel were my personal tools of choice.

The adults participated in an adult coffee hour while the boys participated in a rock wall climbing competition. Joe, one of the adults in our group, got a cup of ice for the first time in a long time and was in heaven! Our boys did very well in the rock wall climbing competition and had a good time.

Day 12 – We got a great start on the day and arrived in Clarks Fork early. This allowed us to play horseshoes and chess. Several of our boys went on a horse ride. They admitted it was a bit anti-climatic after all we had been through. Some of the boys admitted to falling asleep while riding the horses. We also saw B1 Bombers flying overhead.

I had never seen one in person and they are very impressive. We ate lunch at Clarks Fork. I suppose we were all getting a bit giddy from being on the trail for so long. We all started laughing and some of us were laughing so hard that we were crying! The topic of our conversation was the Laura Bars provided to us for our lunch. They looked like poop!

We then hiked the rest of the way to our camp for the evening. The rain started shortly after lunch and continued through the night. When we talked to the staff about the weather, they stated that this was the most rain they had seen in a long time.

We took another opportunity to sit back and reflect on where we were and all of the beauty that surrounded us. We hit the sack early since we had a big day ahead of us as we head back to base camp.

Day 13 - We got up at 3:30 a.m. in an attempt to catch the sunrise from the top of Schaffer Mountain. We were on the trail by 4:40 a.m. This was our quickest time for getting out of camp in the morning. It was kind of spooky hiking at night. Some of the boys felt we were being followed. It could have been that a mountain lion was following us! We did get the bonus of seeing the moon set on our hike up to Schaffer Mountain. Both the moon setting and the sun rising were quite beautiful!

We then proceeded to hike to the top of the Tooth of Time where the view was simply awesome. The climb to the top was like a boulder climb where you jump from huge boulder to huge boulder. Once we got to the top we were a little bit winded. I was surprised to find chipmunks living on the top since there was absolutely no vegetation. We then climbed down from the Tooth of Time and proceeded to base camp. There were many beautiful rock formations. The trail was a bit amusing since it was a switchback. The term "switchback" is used for a trail that zig-zags back and forth rather than heading straight down a hill. The trail is set up this way to help minimize erosion. The funny thing was that for about three hours, we zig-zagged back and forth and kept seeing the base camp down the hill and off in the distance. We would pass the camp and then turn around and head back just to see the camp again. It seemed so close and yet it was so far away.

We came to the end of our journey through the wilderness of Philmont and made it to base camp. I considered it ok with me if I didn't see another dehydrated pineapple for a couple of weeks (or possibly months). Once in camp everyone was buying gifts, using real toilets, and eating junk food from the snack shop. Some of the boys went a bit overboard with the snacks and soda. They were all giddy and I am sure it was the sugar high they were experiencing from the food. Their bodies hadn't experienced a lot of sugar for the past two weeks, so they needed to adjust. About an hour later, these same boys fell asleep while waiting for our lunch at a local pizza shop in downtown Cimmarron. Please note that I use the term "Downtown Cimmarron" loosely. Downtown Cimmarron can be described as very, very small. It consists of a pizza shop, an ice cream parlor, and a bunch of shops that sold knives, colored rocks, knives, pelts, and knives.

The sky that night was a brilliant red color. It was almost fire engine red. I have never seen a sky like that. The closing campfire was held inside due to inclement weather. There were jokes about the adult leaders taking naps, talking on cell phones, and taking lots of pictures. They were dead on.

Day 14 – Still getting up at 5:00 a.m. but that was ok. We had breakfast at the base camp dining hall. They had real bananas and I was pretty sure we were in heaven. We climbed onboard a bus once again. We made a tourist stop at the Cripple Creek Railroad then got back on the bus to go the airport, got on the plane, and made the flight home. We arrived shortly after midnight.

For me, some of the highlights of the trip were:

- Laughter about the Laura Bars at Clarks Fork
- Watching the boys identify problems and solve them
- God's tremendous beauty all around us

It is funny to mention that this chapter is one of the longest in this book. However, the words here do not do this experience justice. It was the hardest chapter to write since it was the most difficult to describe.

Enjoying the amazing Philmont experience with Ryan was a highlight of my life

Chapter 23

What's a Gamer?

Who's with Me?!?

I'm a gamer! At least I am now. I didn't intend to become one, but … well, I am getting a bit ahead of myself …

When I first took off from work, I busted my rear end around the house. I was non-stop for about sixteen hours a day. After doing this for about a year, I realized that I needed a release. What could I do? I kept seeing commercials on television for this game called 'Medal of Honor,' and it looked really cool. The game had lots of action and things to shoot. The thought of working my way through various battle scenarios and wiping out the enemy intrigued me. The next thing I know I am buying a GameCube system and the first game I bought, (of course), was Medal of Honor. I bought the guide book for the game to assist me in case I got stuck, (which I did on numerous occasions).

I read the manual and tried to memorize what each key on the handheld pad did. There was walking forward, walking backward, turning, jumping, stooping, lying down, switching weapons, throwing grenades, aiming, and shooting. There was a lot of stuff going on here, but I thought I had it. I was ready for the next step which was to try the game.

Ready for my First Mission

The first mission was storming the beaches of Normandy. It was really intense. There were bombs going off all around me. There were Germans shooting M32 machine guns from several bunkers on top of the hill and, of course, the snipers. I cannot tell you how many times I died trying to complete this mission. It was intense. Sometimes Ryan would watch me play. He would offer constructive criticism, but I found myself being taken over by the game. I would play until the wee hours of the morning and wouldn't notice when someone came into the room. It was truly addictive!

After playing several different types of games, I continued to enjoy the single-person shooter games. What I did not enjoy were some of the various features found on some of the games. Some games do not allow you free rein to explore. In other words, they pull you through the game and you have to accomplish things when the opportunity presents itself. I did not like the feature where I would get stuck and couldn't proceed no matter what I tried. This happened to me in some James Bond games where they wanted you to use some kind of specific gizmo to open a secret code. I would spend hours in a room trying to figure this out.

Another scenario that I would occasionally get stuck in was where the mission was so intense I couldn't survive no matter what I tried. My frustration would just increase when I would toss the controller to my son. Much to my amazement and frustration, he would typically get through it on the first try with no problem. On the other hand, sometimes a game was too easy. If you want a sense of accomplishment this would have been good, but I wanted a sense of value, too. So when you spend $50 for a game, you want it to last for more than a couple of hours!!

Probably one of the best releases in these games is the head-to-head mode where you fight others. Typically, you are placed in one of the areas associated with a mission from the regular game and then you seek out the other player and try to "neutralize" him. You learn tricks in each of these games that help you go on to master a variety of missions. I spent many an hour playing my son with both of us laughing the whole time!

Chapter 24

Technology Blows

Allow Me to Set the Stage

The stage needs to be set prior to beginning my highly opinionated rant in this chapter. I am ***not*** against technology. In fact, I like to think that I am conservatively guarded when it comes to technology. I understand the need for technology and, as an engineer, I am fascinated by the possibilities. I remember when the cell phone first came out and all I could think was that I could be standing out in the middle of some field in Pennsylvania talking to someone standing in a field all the way across the world without any "hard" connections. I was flabbergasted!

That's not where my fascination stopped. I was sad to see the demise of the vinyl record, but pleased at how small CDs were and how the clarity was truly wonderful. Apple's iPod is simply awesome. It is about the size of a stick of gum and can hold thousands of songs. I remember purchasing one for my wife for Christmas, getting her the 16-gig model. I was shocked to see the 160-gig iPod which can hold up to 40,000 songs, 200 hours of video, or 25,000 photos. It is hard for me to wrap my mind around the size of the device versus the amount it can store.

Talking about storage, I remember the Commodore 64 computer which had 64 megabytes of memory. This was followed by the 286 and then the 386, with the number representing the megabytes of memory. My employers were constantly trying to upgrade their computers to keep up with the demands placed on us by our clients. Eventually, computers made it into gigabytes called "Gigs," and the conversation at the water cooler was about who was going to get the new monster computer. It has been several years since I bought my last computer, so I was totally blown away when they introduced me to a computer with one terabyte which is equivalent to 1,000 gigabytes. (By the time this book is published, I am sure that all of these incredible advances will all be considered archaic)!

How Far We've Come

It does not stop with just the computers. Now we can buy a portable device that we can stick to the windshield of our car and it will talk to us and tell us how to get to our destination. Incredible! Even television has gone through the stratosphere. When I was a kid, there were three VHF stations (referred to as "The Big Three") and one UHF station. Our choices were limited, and some nights we just turned off the TV because nothing good was on. Now we have over two hundred stations and there is always something good on, provided we are willing to spend seventeen minutes flipping through every channel to see what is on. (And this assumes we spend five seconds on each station to see if it is something we want to watch).

The televisions themselves are quite impressive. The day of the "tube" TV are gone and have been replaced with plasma screens, high definition, as well as projection TVs. To watch the Super Bowl in your neighbor's basement on a crystal clear image that is eight feet by ten feet is simply astounding! They even have 3-D televisions, and I am not sure what that means. Does it mean that you are on the set while they are shooting the show?!?

Another thing that amazes me is that we can purchase and watch any movie in our home whenever we want. I vaguely remember as a kid that the only ways to see a movie were going to the movie theater or catching one on TV if we were lucky.

We can also entertain ourselves by playing games on our computer or through a gaming system. The only games I played as a kid were board games (such as Monopoly, Risk,

Battleship, Stratego, Sub Search, Scrabble, Parcheesi, Dominos, Tiddly Winks, and Trouble), cards, or running around in our backyard playing football, stick ball, hide and seek or "smear the queer." Those types of activities do not seem to apply to our current generation of kids. Now we can play interactive video games on our TV or online with people from all over the world. Who needs Scrabble? ...

Some Downsides

There is a downside to all of this incredible technology. The first is the cost. I remember a cartoon that struck a chord with me when I was a young man. It stated that technological devices were developed to save us time but they do cost money. So what do we do with that extra time that technology gives us? The answer seems to be that we work more to have more money to buy more technological devices so we can save more time, so we can work more so we can buy more technological devices. Do you see a pattern here? I cringe at the prospect of my kids going out into the "real world" and trying to accessorize their lives with those things that are deemed "necessary" while trying to survive.

There is so much to consider. There is the cable TV which is a modest $63 per month. (In our house we keep costs down by not getting the expanded package deal). You cannot get an individual cell phone plan for less than $40 per month. If you want the texting or "data" (we are still not sure what the "data" charges are on our one family bill) plan, then you must pay an additional $10 per month. Internet access is $40 per month and satellite radio is $10 per month along with the $10 per month bill for your car's navigation system. If you look at the cable, cell phone, and Internet access alone, it works out to be over $1,800 per year in after-tax dollars. Let's not forget the hardware needed to keep all of this up and running. You are going to need the big HD plasma screen TV, the DVD player, and the surround sound system. There's the gaming system (or two) along with controllers, guns, nunchucks, steering wheels, and games that go for $60 a pop. Your computer, which can easily cost you $2,000 will need to be replaced every couple of years, and don't forget that you will need to upgrade your spyware software to prevent unwanted viruses from attacking your computer. Cell phones seem to last about two years. When you purchase one, you will need to purchase a new charger, ear phones, and carrier (of course). The iPods seem to last two to three years. You won't buy your CDs and DVDs all at once, but I am sure everyone wants to continuously buy them to update their collections. After paying for all of these services and devices, then we will see if there is enough left over to pay for the rent/mortgage, electric bill, water bill, food, clothing, car payments, and insurance which are the real "necessities."

The technology of today can be overwhelming. I remember the day when you would receive all of your communication from someone stopping over your house to talk, a letter in the mail, or a phone call. It should be noted that you didn't typically get all phone calls since that was relying on someone taking a message when you weren't home! Anyway, the first major additional advancement that came along recently was the answering machine. This device ensured that we didn't miss any of our messages (assuming no one accidentally erased them)! The cell phone came next. Now we could be reached at home or instantaneously since we could carry our cell phones with us at all times and people could not only leave messages on our home voicemail, but also on our cell phone. Somewhere in this technological timeline came the fax machine where people from all over the world could send us documents over the phone lines. When e-mail came along, the world changed again. Another level of complexity is added to our lives. I don't know about you, but after I have read through all of the mail and listened to all of my home voicemail messages, the last thing I want to do is to sit down to the computer and spend another forty-five minutes going through all of my e-mails.

Another problem for me is that when I quit my job to become "Mr. Mom," I did not want to sit in front of the computer checking e-mails. As a result, I started falling behind since I only checked them once every week or so. This got me in big trouble. I remember checking my e-mails one day and finding one that referenced a meeting that had occurred the previous day. I had totally missed the meeting! This situation stressed me out quite a bit since I am not one to take meetings casually. Anyway, now I try to check e-mails on a regular basis to stay out of trouble. Let's not forget the blogs, chat rooms, and Instant Messaging that I am bombarded with whenever I am online. A couple of years ago, Facebook started up and I felt all of this pressure to open up my own account. (I am not even going to mention Twitter). I couldn't help but think to myself, "What am I going to give up in order to devote the time that's needed to maintain all of these communication devices? When am I going to eat?"

Have We Really Saved Time and Money?

The more technology we have in our lives the more maintenance that needs to be done. This maintenance takes time and more money. I have a great story to demonstrate this point. Our computer started to give us problems. I had to break down and disconnect our CPU so that I could take it in to be diagnosed. The store took a look at it and determined I had a bad virus so they cleaned it up. I paid $170, brought the CPU home, and hooked it all back up again. Everything worked well for a couple of weeks. Then it started acting up again. I took it back to the same establishment, at which point they looked it over and said it was fine. They were kind enough not to bill me, but within a couple of days, the computer was acting up again. I decided to take it to a different place. This time the computer would not even let you get to a menu so I was a little frightened. I took it in and they said they would diagnose it. They determined the computer was "fried," and that I needed to buy another one. I decided to buy a new CPU but to keep my old printer and monitor as I had done in the past. I also decided not to fool around, and I got the "monster" computer which would supposedly last us several years. All of the necessary software was downloaded onto the computer and the data from the old computer was transferred to the new computer. I paid $970, took it home, and hooked it up. All was well until I went to hook up the printer. Long story short … the old cable that ran between the printer and the previous computer would not work with the new computer. I went back to the store and determined that there were a lot of different adapter cables but none that met my needs. So you will never guess what I had to do. That's right! I had to buy a new printer.

The sales representative told me that the hook-up was easy and I should have no problem. I paid the $160, took it home and hooked it up. When I went to download the software that came with the computer, a message appeared on my screen stating that the computer had a platform not recognized by the software. One option was that I could download the software online. However, I knew that this truly was not an option since I have had horrible experiences with this in the past. It was time to bring in a professional which I did. He did an excellent job and charged me $150 for his services. While he was there, we brought it to his attention that our monitor was giving off a high-pitched whining noise. He informed us that we should consider getting a new monitor. I fought off this notion for a couple of weeks but finally broke down and spent another $160 on a new monitor when we just couldn't take it any longer. At this point everyone is happy with our new computer, but was it worth the $2,000 and countless hours of effort? Only time will truly tell ...

I find myself asking many questions any time a new gizmo comes into my life. Now, I am a firm believer that simpler is better, but there are those that believe differently. I remember the last time I bought a cell phone and wanted a simple phone. I was looking for a phone that could receive and send calls. All of the phones in the store had built-in cameras. I would have to place a special order to get a phone without a camera. So I placed my order and I finally received my new phone. I took it home and began reading the 400-page owners' manual. I gave up after two hours and decided to just wing it. I would say that I understand about ten percent of what the phone is capable of. The good news is that I know how to make and receive phone calls. The bad news is that I am not sure how to remove the permanent message my kids placed on the phone's screen stating "You smell funny."

To Quote my Wise Grandfather

"If it ain't broke, don't fix it" is what my grandfather used to say and I tend to agree with him. Can anyone please explain to me why the software companies think they need to change everything when they create an upgraded version of their software? It really aggravates me when I have just mastered some software and then the upgrade comes along. The first time I use the software I go to execute a command only to find that it is now done differently. It is like they are forcing me to forget everything I learned in the past and to start fresh. I can tell you that this old mind is only going to be able to do that so many times.

So what do I really think about technology? It has become a necessary evil. Our society is forcing us to use the latest and greatest, and it isn't just to "keep up with the Joneses." It is becoming necessary to meet the daily demands and to function successfully. My biggest fear is that the distance between the "have's" and the "have not's" is getting greater. A perfect example of this concern is when I was a civil engineer making presentations at public meetings. At the end of most meetings, we would inform the local community that additional information could be found on the website for the project and there would be updates as well as opportunities for them to weigh in on what was going on. I would ask other members of the team how community members would access this information if they did not have a computer (because believe it or not ... not everyone has a computer with Internet access). The response to my question was that they could go to the local library and use the computers. I had to laugh because:
(1) I know that not all libraries have adequate computer facilities, (2) Not everyone has reasonable access to a library, and (3) Not everyone has time to get to the library to stay involved. It was a poor assumption.

Chapter 25

Put Me In, Coach

Always a Learning Experience

As you know I have volunteered in many ways throughout the years. This includes coaching kids in a variety of sports. Ryan has been in basketball, soccer, baseball, lacrosse, and even Tae Kwon Do. This has created all kinds of opportunities for me to get involved. I would always let Ryan's coaches know that I was available to assist in any way they saw fit. I figured I was there anyway, so I may as well help out. As a result of my over-eagerness, I would lead soccer drills, run around the basketball court coaching the kids, hit thousands of grounders and pop flies, pitch hundreds of pitches, act as base coach, and provide general moral support.

It was fun, but I did make a couple of major mistakes along the way. I remember one night receiving a phone call at my house asking where I was. The answer to that question was obvious since they called me at home but I decided to play along. I told them I was at home and then I asked who they were and why they were asking me where I was. It was then explained to me that I was one of the head soccer coaches in Ryan's soccer league and there was a coaches meeting at the elementary school. Well I immediately knew that a horrible mistake had been made. You see, there is no way I would have volunteered to be head coach because that meant that I would have to be at all of the practices as well as games. At that point in my life I had numerous nighttime commitments so I could not properly commit to being head coach. Then it dawned on me. I vaguely remembered checking off the box stating that I would volunteer to be an ***assistant*** coach. The way I had figured it, I was already fulfilling that role so I may as well check off the box. Well, I believe that by checking off the assistant coach box on Ryan's registration form I was essentially telling the recreation council that I was willing to be ***head*** coach. That moment was a learning experience for me. I learned that it is better to just show up and help out versus letting anyone know up front that you are willing.

I did enjoy helping Ryan's various teams learn skills as well as how to work together to meet a goal. A couple of his teams actually did really well. However, there were certain aspects of the experience that did not make sense to me. A big example of this is the concept that everyone gets trophies no matter how well the team did. I clearly remember the trophy ceremony for Ryan's league. There were probably eight teams. Some teams had done remarkably well, while others had ... well ... **not** done remarkably well. It seemed that it did not matter how well the kids performed, since all of the kids got the same trophy. In other words if the boy's team had no losses, they got the same reward as the teams who did not win a single game. This was true in all of the sports Ryan played and was clearly demonstrated in the lacrosse experience that Ryan had.

My Philosophy

When I talked to the various organizers, they stated that by giving all the kids trophies, nobody's feelings are hurt. I am strongly against this philosophy. It sets a poor precedent and hurts the kids in the long run. We need to prepare our children to be able to eventually go out on their own and function in our society. It has been my experience that when you succeed you are rewarded, and when you perform poorly, you are not rewarded. Why shouldn't it be the same for recreational sports? Sure it is okay to give a certificate or a small medallion, but not a trophy to those who performed poorly. We shouldn't reward failure. We should encourage success.

Chapter 26

Really?!?

Television Then and Now

Television has come a long way since I was a kid. In the beginning of my childhood, the televisions were black and white. Now, I am pretty sure that today's generation does not even know what a black and white television is. We didn't have a television remote control. Compared to today's standards, it was almost criminal to think about how you would have to get up out of your seat to change the channel every single time you wanted to see what the alternatives were. For some families the "remote control" was the youngest member of the family who sat closest to the television and had the job of changing it to different stations. The good news was that back then there were only a few channels to check out. There were the "Big Three" - CBS, NBC, and ABC. You would find these on the VHF stations. Here in Baltimore we had a couple of UHF stations as well. There was channel 45 out of Baltimore and, if the weather conditions were perfect, you could catch channel 54 out of Washington, DC (but you didn't count on it)! The choices were pretty limited.

That is not the case today. Many families now have cable or satellite which consists of over one hundred stations. I am not exactly sure how many stations our family has, but I once hit too many buttons on the remote control and was pleasantly surprised to learn that we have a channel 446. What does this mean? Well, in my opinion, it means that there is room for a lot of junk out there. As a stay-at-home dad, I was able to witness some of the junk that exists. After experiencing some of it firsthand, it turns out that my opinion just might be right.

The Goodies

Now don't get me wrong. There is some good programming on television nowadays. There are the funny shows that have the ability to make us laugh. One of my favorites is the show "Whose Line Is It Anyway?" The show consists of four comedians doing improvisational comedy. The cost to do the show has to be close to nothing. Besides the four comedians, the set consists of chairs, tables, and boxes of props. These comedians are immensely talented and extremely funny. It is my opinion that it is the best kind of television there is. I also enjoy a good sitcom. When good actors collide with good writers, the end result is simply astounding. Some of the best sitcoms of all time include "Seinfeld," "Cheers," "The Cosby Show," "Everybody Loves Raymond," and "Modern Family." All of these shows tickle my funny bone!

Another form of good television is when it is used for educational purposes. The Learning Channel and the History Channel fill my mind with all kinds of interesting information. Television becomes an enormously powerful tool when used to educate. It is sad to see that only a handful of the hundreds of channels available fit into this category. I also believe television is a great tool to bring the arts into our home. Whether it is a concert or a Broadway play, it is a great tool to introduce people, especially children, to various forms of the arts. Finally, there are sports. Television can capture a sporting event and allow viewers to embrace the event. For instance, my family loves watching the Olympics from thousands of miles away.

... And the Less-Than-Stellar (Ok, Bad) Ones

A lot of the rest of the programming that can be found on television is truly c--p (pardon my French). Since I believe that television plays a large role in developing our perceptions, the load of c--p we see has a huge negative impact on our society. It impacts us as individuals, couples, and as families. When provided the opportunity of time and there is a choice to be made between television and let's say playing a board game with our family, we will typically choose television since it somehow consumes us. It is my opinion that the times where television is chosen are, for the most part, lost moments. You can ask me what I watched on television last night and I probably cannot tell you. However, if you asked me about when I played board games with my family, I can honestly tell you that there were times where we laughed until we cried. These are memories worth holding onto. It is my opinion that we create the most meaningful memories through our interactions with others.

Unfortunately, there is a lot of bad television programming. Some of it promotes stupidity, while others knock marriage which I believe is one of the cornerstones of our society. A lot of television gives false impressions or promotes poor choices. Some programs create drama that really isn't there. The biggest culprit seems to be "Reality TV" which does not seem to be based on reality at all!

The programs that promote stupidity, or are just plain stupid, are too numerous to list. I do have some favorites that deserve to be mentioned. It is my opinion that these shows should be banned. They promote others going out and doing the same thing. I remember as a child that I came up with plenty of stupid ideas on my own; I did not need a source of never-ending material to give me new ideas! Some of the sources include the video shows that show people making poor choices time and again. Sometimes the participants suffer horrific consequences as a result. "Jackass," the television series (that went onto movies), is truly alarming. Here are a group of people trying to intentionally create dangerous situations and then carry them out! The show "Redneck Wedding" is a show that promotes stereotypical views of people from the South. The show has couples participating in crazy weddings that feature such things as cakes made of cheese, mud wrestling, and lots of beer drinking. Another aspect of the show that is a turn-off for me is that the show belittles marriage and most couples don't seem to have a lot of respect for one another.

Other stupid programming includes shows like "Parking Wars." This is a show where the cameras follow the stories from local parking districts. Let me put this another way, ... it is a show where you can watch very angry people try to pay their parking tickets or get their cars back after being towed. I just have to shake my head as I ponder how this ever became a television show to begin with. How about the show that has toddlers in beauty pageants? Let me repeat that ... toddlers in beauty pageants. The show is very controversial and I ***cannot*** imagine why!?! Who would not want to watch mothers forcing their pre-school kids to walk down the runway and to demonstrate a talent? I guess these parents do not realize that their kids look to them to help form their values. Maybe if they thought about what they were doing from that perspective, they would stop screaming at their kids and just let them be kids. They can pursue the parents' dreams when they get a little bit older.

<u>Another Example of 'Really'?!?</u>
Marriage is a topic that I hold near and dear to my heart. I am a strong advocate of marriage, so when I see our society trying to tear it down, it makes me a bit crazy. We should be promoting the commitment that marriage requires instead of equating relationships to being expendable.

The first television show that I recall busting on marriage was "Married with Children." The wife used the husband while the husband detested his wife. Many people thought it was funny, but it was sending a message that marriage was something that didn't have to be respected. Cultivating a good marriage is difficult enough without everyone around you being against it. When it first came out, I refused to watch it. Little did I know that this was just the tip of the iceberg when it came to shows belittling marriage. The premise of the television reality show "Temptation Island" was so bizarre that when I first heard about it, I did not believe it was true. Not only was it true, but the show was around for three years and shown in numerous countries. For those of you who may not remember what it was all about, here is the premise: Several couples agreed to live with a group of singles of the opposite sex in order to test their relationships. In other words the show was trying to destroy relationships. Really?!?

It seems to me that there are all sorts of shows where everyone is sleeping with everyone else and where relationships are totally expendable. The latest one that I can think of is "Desperate Housewives." This show has been running for eight seasons. It is classified as a comedy-drama, but I don't hear anyone laughing. The show has featured wives having affairs on their husbands, surprise children appearing from a husband, divorce, wives having affairs with their ex-husbands, teenagers with illegitimate children, sons having affairs with married women, and a wife experimenting with her sexuality, just to name a few of the story lines amongst what appears to be a very dysfunctional neighborhood!

It is very ironic that they call the recent new format of television programming "Reality TV" when it doesn't appear to based in reality at all. Let's use the "Real Housewives" series. First, there were the "Real Housewives of Orange County," followed by the "Real Housewives of New York City," followed by the "Real Housewives of Atlanta," which was followed by the "Real Housewives of New Jersey," then the "Real Housewives of Beverly Hills," and finally, the "Real Housewives of Miami." Let's not forget the "Real Housewives of D.C." or the "Real Housewives of Athens" which have both come and gone.

Heck, this epidemic of poor television has even gone international. There is the "Real Housewives of Israel" and the "Real Housewives of Vancouver."

Not to Leave out the Spin-offs

Let's not forget the spin-offs! There is "Date My Ex" that spun off from "Real Housewives of Orange County." "Bethany Ever After..." is a spin-off from "Real Housewives of New York City." Both "The Kandi Family" and "Don't be Tardy for the Wedding" are spin-offs from "Real Housewives of Atlanta." The show "Sur" spun off from "Real Housewives of Beverly Hills." All of this cropped up overnight and became a huge sensation. Now it appears that I am a big fan of the "Real Housewives" series when you look at all of my fancy statistics. However, what is really amazing is what you can find on the Internet! I have watched the show to see what all of hubbub was all about. In the shows I watched, the premise is about women who are married to very, very wealthy husbands. They live in palatial homes in gated communities. They wear jewelry worth more than most Americans will make in a lifetime. They wear the finest clothes and eat the best food available. I have to just scratch my head wondering, "Is this reality?" This group of people represents the top 0.0001% of our population. I don't know anyone who lives like this, and I believe that this onslaught of shows gives us false impressions of how we think we are supposed to live. I have to admit that the shows are about these rich people's lives, as they simply sent a cameraman in amongst their lives to film all of their intimate details. Then we sit back and watch what the editors want to show us and really miss out on having lives of our own.

"Teen Mom" is another reality television show that gives me the willies. This show is a spin-off of "16 and Pregnant." Either way, they are shows that feature teenage girls struggling through pregnancy and then coping with a newborn baby. This show was being watched by teenage girls all over the nation, who were probably inspired to become pregnant themselves, to maybe be featured on this twisted reality television show. It is my opinion that shows like these promote poor choices such as getting pregnant when someone is so young. How about a show featuring the struggles with abstinence?

In the Loop

I believe that the news gives us misleading and even false impressions. News shows would have you believe that the entire planet is basically on fire and that it is a strong possibility all of us will be murdered or, at the very least, assaulted. I have been trapped many times in situations where there is a television with one of the 24-7 all news stations on. I noticed that these stations do two things very well: They enjoy creating anxiety for their viewers, and they seem to want to show these stories to us again and again and again. That is why I call it the "Loop of Terror."

Where I think it all Started

Some reality shows are just in it for the drama. They go out of their way to create the drama, or they edit the film that they took to put a dramatic spin on it. I just sit there and shake my head in total amazement and bewilderment.

I guess reality television started with the MTV show "Real World." I remember when MTV was about showing music videos. Now, it seems to me that a majority of MTV consists of reality shows inspired by "Real World." The show was supposed to be about young adults coping with being young adults. It throws a group of strangers together in the same house and then turns on the cameras and lets the drama unfold. I watched it once and almost got sick to my stomach. The show featured a bunch of ill-tempered, foul-mouthed, drunk, sloppy, prejudiced, promiscuous and irresponsible young adults. I am sure that the parents of these kids were shocked to see their children behave this way. This show also proved what the presence of a camera can do to people. It is clear that much of the drama was developed because there was an opportunity to be dramatic in front of the whole world. I say, "Shut up and get out there and do something with your lives!"

This theme carried on in the reality show "Jersey Shore." In many ways, this show has become more popular, but to me it is just as disturbing. The show is full of false information which has led to more drama. Not all the cast is from New Jersey. Six of the nine cast members come from New York and one comes from Rhode Island. The show was advertised as a collection of "Guido's" and "Guidette's." This has created a lot of controversy since this term is considered to be an ethnic slur referring to Italians and Italian-Americans. All of the cast members are not Italian but have roots in other countries including Chile, Spain, and Ireland. The Governor of New Jersey actually criticized the show as well. And why not?!? The show is full of disturbing actions - these young adults drink, fight, have their breasts enlarged, have sex, curse, get arrested, and well, let's just say they are not the people we want to have as role models for our children.

"Wife Swap" is a very interesting premise for a reality show, and it is all about creating drama. The name of the show itself conjures up controversy as wife swapping implies a popular party activity in the late 1960's where couples would get together and switch partners for the evening. This show doesn't do that, but it is just as crazy. It seems that the producers for the show scour the country looking for married couples with very strong values who are willing to be on a television show. What they do is match up couples with very different sets of values. For instance, they will have one family who is all about hunting and another family who is all about gun control. Another example is the wife who puts all of her eggs into the basket of bringing up her children swapped with a wife who does not put a lot of credence into raising kids. One of my favorites is the wife who is meticulous around the household going to a family who puts cleaning at the bottom of their "to do" list. Another favorite is the family who does not ask their children to help out around the house while another family has their kids working from sunup to sundown. Or how about this scenario, where a wife from an ultra-conservative family is swapped with a wife from a radically-liberal family? It seems that no stone is left unturned as they explore swapping wives between families with different religious beliefs, demographics, financial status ... you name it, this show has been there.

Then there are shows about essentially nothing. The show "Keeping Up with the Kardashians" is an example of the show that fits into this category. To sum up the experience...who cares? I don't care who is getting a tattoo where. I don't care who is going to prison. I don't care who is marrying whom or who is divorcing whom. It is a show about a family that has been made famous because of the show. Once again, it is an example of the viewer watching something about someone else's life instead of living their own.

Instilling Positive Messages

As a stay-at-home dad, I got more exposure to the poor programming that is found on television. I learned to try to be selective in what I watch as well as to guide my children toward programming that was informative or entertaining in a positive and uplifting way. For television shows where the material was a bit controversial, I would make it a point to talk about it after the show was over. I wanted to make sure that what my children saw on television was not necessarily acceptable behavior.

The other part of the equation is the amount of television watched. Television has a way of sucking me in and not letting go. I have tried to make a conscious decision to disengage from the TV, and instead to reach out to my family to encourage other activities like going for a walk, going out to eat, or playing a board game. It is through these efforts that I believe I have been able to create meaningful memories that will last a lifetime.

Chapter 27

I'll Give You a Quarter

Who Wants to Make a Deal?

I love to go to flea markets, have garage sales, and sell stuff at swap meets. There are certain types of people who attend these events and I find each one fascinating.

There are the people looking for the "deal." They are hoping to stumble upon that item that is worth a lot and get it for a little. I guess you could say they are looking for a diamond in a mountain of rocks. I try to cater to these buyers. It took a while, but I found that you shouldn't be totally organized when it comes to yard sales. So I always have several boxes that people need to root through to find anything. Personally, I would find this to be a bit aggravating, but they do not seem to mind. In fact, they seem to thrive on this situation. They will spend a good half-hour looking through boxes of books or a box of kids' toys. They develop a mindset that there has to be a diamond in this box somewhere.

Of course, there are the people who like to haggle. No matter how cheap the asking price, they enjoy the thrill of talking you down. My personal preference is to price everything to sell. For instance, I priced a Barbie playhouse, which cost $250 brand new for $20. Someone showed up and said they would give me $15. I guess I should have asked for $25 so that I would have gotten the $20 I was looking for.

Then there was the one time a couple of friends and I went to a car show where we participated in a swap meet. We were selling a couple of really serious items such as transmissions, engines, rear ends, as well as complete cars. We had rented a parcel van to haul everything there. We also had smaller items for sale as well. One teenage kid kept stopping by to check out a set of small speakers we had on sale for $2. He must have stopped by at least five times that day. Well, it was the last day of the four-day show. We had done pretty well, but we hadn't sold everything. So there we are busting our backs loading up these engines and rear ends, and this kid finally makes his bid of $1 on the speakers. There was just so much to laugh about in this scenario. For one thing, we were only asking $2. Second, if we had no problem loading hundreds of pounds of car parts, we were certainly not going to have any problem loading those measly speakers!

Early Birds

There are the people who live for yard sales, and they know that the early bird gets the worm. When setting a time for a yard sale, you always want to give yourself enough time to set up. I have found that if you start setting up around 6:30 a.m., you can be ready by 9:00. It never fails that someone will show up around two hours before the advertised time. They will start rooting through your boxes as you are unpacking them. So I am not only dealing with the overwhelming thought that there is no way I can get this set up in time, but I am falling over this person who is constantly getting in my way. I get a bit perturbed thinking that if I wanted them to be at my house at 7:00 a.m., then I would have invited them to be there that early. Instead I bite my tongue.

And then there are the people who just want to spend money. I guess they feel fulfilled by the amount they buy. I remember one gentleman coming in and just piling stuff I had for sale into a box. It appeared that I had everything he wanted. I really believe that he did not know what he wanted. He wanted to just spend some money. I have also experienced this at the end of car shows. It will be the last day of the show and patrons will start heading toward the gate as the show is ending. Well they just have to buy something! If you are selling relatively inexpensive stuff, you will be in luck. They will stop in and buy something just so they can feel the sense of accomplishment. They are thinking to themselves, "I have come and I have conquered!"

Sometimes You Just Have to Laugh

Then there are the people who buy things that they have no way to take home. This is especially true for the big items. I once had some bar stools for sale at a very reasonable price. They sold quickly (I guess my price was a bit too reasonable), but this lady did not have a way to get them home. I offered to drive them to her house and found myself in a position where I was going to spend as much in gas as I had made from the sale. How do I get myself in these situations?!?

The people who don't know when to stop always make me chuckle. Picture this: I am sitting out in my yard. Basically I have on display all of the stuff that I consider not worthy to spend any more time on in my house. In a way, it is humiliating. Well, just when you think it cannot get worse, you are proven wrong. I once had a woman come up to me and ask me how much I was willing to sell the ferns that were in my flower beds. Lady, I am not selling my shrubs, but I am willing to negotiate on this pair of oven mitts.

Kids like to spend money, too. I found that placing a box of toys right where the people pay is a good idea. The kids always see the toys and typically convince their parents to make a purchase on their behalf.

Getting Involved Myself

I started a small business selling used car magazines. I would purchase old car magazines, check their condition, price them based on their condition and age, and then go to local car shows. Now there are numerous vendors at car shows who already do this, so I needed to find a niche. I decided to catalogue the magazines. What this means is that I would go through each magazine page by page, and anytime I would find an article featuring a specific car, I would enter it into a database. The idea is that someone could approach me and ask if I had an article featuring the car they are looking for and I could find it. (Yeah, I need a hobby). Anyway I cannot tell you how many people I overwhelm by this approach. I truly believe that people don't believe that I can do what I claim to be able to do. I had one gentleman come in and ask if I had any articles on a 1973 Dodge Challenger. Now those of you who know cars will know that this is a relatively rare car. The cars that magazines cover are the ones that are high-profile or high-power cars. This car was neither. I did the research for him and within minutes I had a beautiful multi-page article that had a two-page color spread on the car. In addition, it was a vintage article, which means it was featured in a magazine from 1973. Well he just stood there dumbfounded. He didn't know what to do so he walked away. I guess I am just too good at what I do.

Since starting up this business I have unusual interactions with the people purchasing my magazines. At a recent show, I had a surreal experience dealing with other vendors. My goal at these car shows is to sell as many magazines as possible to cover the cost of the show and make a profit. Well, at this show I had vendors coming to me and assessing how I ran my business. They would sit and talk to me while I was trying to attract customers. (I found that I need to educate potential patrons on what I can do because it isn't obvious from my displays). These vendors would be doing this while they left their booth unattended. I am no expert, but I am pretty sure you cannot make a sale unless you are at your booth! One vendor took it as far as watching me interact with a customer and then critiquing my performance afterwards. I didn't have the gumption to tell him to get back to his own business and keep his nose out of mine!

Danielle enjoys yard sales, too!

Chapter 28

I Have a Voice

Voting Counts

I remember the conversation very clearly. I was having a "water cooler" discussion with a co-worker and somehow the topic of politics came up. He started to complain about the President at that time, such as not liking what the President stood for or his decisions. After griping continuously for several minutes, I asked him whom he had voted for in the previous election. He informed me that he hadn't voted. I told him to shut up. It is my opinion that voting is one of the many privileges here in the United States, since many countries do not have elections. I also think that everyone should exercise that right. It is important that we try to make a difference in the world and voting is an opportunity to do just that. This co-worker was entitled to his opinion, but when he doesn't vote and try to get the person into office that he thinks will do the better job, then his complaining holds no credence in my book.

Being a Civil Engineer for many years and working on numerous public projects, I have attended many public meetings. I have dealt with enraged people, drunk people, and people whose beliefs had become their realities, no matter how strange. It has been my experience that nine times out of ten, the people who attend these public meetings are those who are against the project. They are upset with the project's impacts or sometimes they fight any project that moves their community forward.

Idea #1 (Hypothetical)

For instance, a new road may be proposed that will improve efficiency in the local community. Thousands of motorists will save time and money every day because of the new road. These motorists are typically not the people who show up at the public meetings. Rather, the people who attend are the ones upset about the relocation of a business, the taking of farmlands, or some other impact. The impacts are real and I understand people's reaction to the projects. However, I also realize that many projects provide huge benefits for the overall community and that some sacrifice is needed to make it happen.

***Idea* #2 (Actual)**

For instance, a developer had a significant parcel in our community which was zoned as residential and could accommodate nine homes. The developer proposed to give one hundred acres of the parcel to the county's recreation council to build a recreational facility. In exchange, the developer asked for permission to build another ten homes for a total of nineteen homes. In this case, the need for athletic fields was huge and the search for property to build more facilities had been going on for years. The problem was so bad that the local recreation council paid about $50,000 per year to rent fields for the lacrosse program at locations about forty-five minutes away. They also had to turn away some kids from the basketball program because there were not enough courts to accommodate all of the teams. There was a real need and the developer's proposal appeared to be a win-win solution. I attended several public meetings regarding the proposed development and read numerous articles about the situation. The people opposed to the project were very organized and spent thousands of dollars fighting the project. They felt the project was too far-reaching, and they just did not want it. After a while, the opposition group finally admitted that there was a problem with the lack of athletic facilities in the area and asked why other sites were not considered. The recreation council members explained that they had been searching for years and this was the best deal to come along. The opposition group offered to assist in finding another site. That was many years ago and sadly, nothing has been built. In this example, the kids lost, the developer lost, and the overall local community lost.

Amazing Assortment of Opportunities

This is a great country and the fact that we can make our voices be heard in a number of different ways is simply amazing. We should take advantage of that. We should provide support for those projects we deem are necessary to move our society forward. There are always impacts, but as long as the compensation for those impacts is fair, then we need to keep advancing. So how can we do this? I have learned over the past several years as a stay-at-home dad that there are numerous ways, some of which take little effort and some that are more significant.

It is important to speak out and let our opinions be known. Here is a list I came up with for ways we can make our voices heard in our communities:

- ✓ Attend local public meetings that discuss the projects going on in our neighborhoods. Since we are the ones who live in our community, we can provide insight directly to the people making decisions in our area. It can help the decisions be more meaningful and to have a positive impact. We cannot be afraid to come out to support what we believe is right.

- ✓ Correspond with our local, state and federal representatives to help them understand our values so they can vote based on what they hear from their constituents. We may see these people at community functions and be able to get some "face time." Constituents' opinions are also solicited through e-mail and even phone calls. I believe it is important to take a little bit of our time and respond. Writing letters directly to representatives or using their websites to give opinions on the issues are other great ways to communicate.

- ✓ Write editorials in response to articles in the local newspaper. I find the articles in the local papers tend to discuss the opposition to a project since these are the people who attend the various public meetings. If I am for the project, I write a short editorial that lets everyone know where I stand on the issue. I believe that every little bit helps and could spur others into speaking up as well.

- ✓ Vote for those who represent the values that you have. I try to educate myself before going to the polls, so that I can vote for the people who I think are best suited for the job. If I cannot find any information regarding their platform, then I do not vote for them. I admit that I made that mistake once and voted for a person who apparently had strong connections to the mob. At that moment I declared to never again go into the voting booth uneducated.

We need to raise our voices so we can be heard. Otherwise, projects and programs with great value may fall to the wayside and never come to fruition. This is not only a tragedy for our generation, but also for generations to come.

Chapter 29

Planes, Trains and Automobiles

"We can laugh about it now. We're all right."

John Candy from the movie "Planes, Trains and Automobiles"

Our Great Tradition

Michele and I have a wonderful anniversary tradition. We alternate years as to who will plan something special, and then we surprise each other with where we are going and what we are doing. We have celebrated in many different ways over the years. There have been the simpler things like going out to dinner or maybe spending the night at a hotel in downtown Baltimore. We have also gone to some very nice places such as Chicago, Boston, Philadelphia, Williamsburg, Cape May, and Block Island. Some of the more elaborate celebrations included going to places such as Cancun, Jamaica, and St. Martin. I love our tradition, since I enjoy planning trips for Michele and surprising her. And on the other hand, I also enjoy being surprised.

Just recently we were celebrating our 25th wedding anniversary and it was Michele's turn to plan the trip. I knew it was a big one, and I tried to guess where we might be going. I thought that anywhere in the Caribbean would be appropriate since we always love it down there and there is so much to do. I also thought about Chicago since it was one of our favorite past celebrations. I was very much surprised when she announced that we would be going to Paris, France. It was an excellent choice, because my brother lived there with his family at the time and that gave us a place to stay. In addition, since Michele and I have been there before on separate trips, we were both somewhat familiar with Paris. We both enjoy walking around and experiencing new things together, so I just knew we were in for a good time. However, we had no idea of what we were getting into from a transportation perspective.

A Sign of Things to Come

Things started out very well. We drove to Washington Dulles International Airport in Virginia, parked our car, and walked half a mile or so to the main terminal. The flight was long but very typical. It wasn't until we landed that things started to go a bit awry. We considered taking a bus, taxi, or train from the Charles De Gaulle Airport to downtown Paris. The taxi was a bit expensive and the train was probably the most direct, so we opted to take the train. After purchasing tickets for the SNCF (Société Nationale des Chemins de Fer), the French national train company, we took our six pieces of luggage to the platform and started to read the various signs to figure out which train went where. Unfortunately, the signs were mostly in French, creating a real language barrier for us. After selecting the train that we thought was the correct one, we boarded. Like most trains, our tickets were not checked until we got on the train.

This created some anxiety since we were not really sure we were on the right train until we were well underway. When the ticket taker hadn't arrived after several minutes, I started to monitor the stations we were stopping at and I compared them to the route map posted on the train. The first couple of stations were under major reconstruction so there were no signs. By the time we saw a sign for one of the stations, it appeared (after a very quick glance), that we were heading away from downtown. A quick decision was needed since the train only stopped for a minute or so. I quickly decided that we were on the wrong train and we needed to get off. I hurriedly gathered our three larger pieces of luggage off of the overhead rack and began to follow Michele to the exit. She waited for me and then stepped off of the train. I began to move down the steps with one piece of luggage in front of me and two behind me. As I was just about to step off the train, the doors slid shut on my hand. So there we were: Michele was standing on the platform and I was in the train with one hand outside holding onto the piece of luggage. Of course the doors wouldn't open, so Michele grabbed the luggage. I retrieved my hand and I told her I would come back to her as the train proceeded to leave the station. I then went back to my seat and pondered our next steps. Looking carefully at the map, I determined we had been going in the right direction. My confusion was rooted in the fact that the transportation map we had been given did not include the airport stop or even most of the stops between the airport and the downtown. To my chagrin I also determined that Michele had my passport, wallet, and all of my cash. We did not have cell phones with us so there was no easy way to communicate. I needed to keep a low profile so I wouldn't get into any trouble with the law! I got off at the next station, crossed the tracks with our luggage, and got onto the train headed in the other direction. While proceeding back, I hoped that Michele hadn't decided to deviate from our plan and would wait for me. You can imagine my joy when I saw she was still there. We then got back on the train (hauling all six pieces of our luggage) and headed into downtown Paris.

We had to get off the SNCF at Notre Dame and switch over to a Metro train. By this time, we were dragging our luggage. The switch went smoothly, and we only had a couple of stops before we had to get off right by my brother's apartment. I was now prone to check the map at every stop to make sure that we were headed in the right direction and did not overshoot our stop. The anticipation of seeing my brother and his family was growing with each stop. When we were one stop away, the train stopped abruptly, the ventilation system shut down, and the lights went off. This did not look promising. That was when the announcement came on that this was the end of the line!

We were a bit shocked and quite exhausted as we lugged our luggage up to the correct platform and took our last train. We got off and towed our luggage the last quarter of a mile. We vowed to take the taxi next time.

Off to Amboise

The next day Michele scheduled an excursion for us to Amboise. It is a beautiful village just south of Paris. We took the Metro to the main train station where we needed to catch another SNCF train. Once there, we were surprised to learn that there was a strike by the mass transit employees. Systems were running but not at full capacity. We had gotten to the station in plenty of time to catch our train; however, that train was not going to run that day due to the strike. A very friendly employee of the SNCF told us about another train we could catch that would get us close to where we were going. He helped us get our tickets and we asked him when and from where the train was leaving. He then pointed to a train that was a couple of platforms over. He kindly explained that it was leaving in three minutes. Michele and I sprinted for the train.

We made it to the train and had a wonderful hour-long trip through the French countryside. Once we arrived at our stop, we learned that the next train to take us on the last leg of our journey would not arrive for five hours or so. The train station was in the middle of a very industrialized area and it was not romantic at all. There was no bus service due to the strike, so the only other alternative was to take a taxi. We put cost aside and said "yes" to the taxi which the friendly station worker arranged for us.

Biking Through the French Countryside

Amboise is quite beautiful. It is a town of tight streets and quaint homes. I love architecture and fell in love with it immediately. The town is situated close to a number of beautiful chateaus. Michele told me that her plan was to rent bicycles and ride out to several of the chateaus the next day. She wanted my opinion on whether we should do sixteen or thirty-two miles of biking.

I have to digress here to discuss an experience when we were first dating. We were eighteen years old and were always in search of cheap entertainment. I loved to bike so I suggested that we bike around my neighborhood. It was in the summer so it was a bit hot that day. We started off and everything was fine—that is, until Michele began to heat up. I didn't know it at the time, but she does not like to sweat. So there she was all sweaty swearing about our cursed excursion.

As a result, as Michele asked for my opinion about a sixteen versus thirty-two-mile bike trip through the French countryside, I immediately said we should opt for the shorter of the two. In addition, I had recently completed a fifty-mile bike trip with two young scouts and it took a good part of the day just to bike that distance. I wanted us to have enough time to enjoy the sights, and I did not want her to get all heated up and upset. My instincts paid off in spades as we headed out of Amboise up a hill that was about a mile long. Michele was cursing about how crazy this was and she was never going to make it. I gently encouraged her and we did make it. It turned out to be a fantastic day.

Traveling Throughout Paris

Throughout the following week, we took the Metro and RER Trains throughout Paris. They go everywhere, which makes them practical. They come frequently, which makes them convenient. And thirdly, they come when the schedule says they will, which makes them efficient. Besides taking mass transportation, we did a lot of walking as well. Michele had a pedometer with her so we kept track of the distance we traveled each day. On our longest day, we walked a little over sixteen miles. That is a lot a miles!

We hated to see it end, but it had to eventually. I had a test in the class that I was taking at the local community college back home and Michele knew that she had to get back to her job.

<u>Unbelievable!</u>

Regrettably, our trip home was a bit more exciting than our arrival trip. We took a taxi and arrived to the airport well before our flight was scheduled to take off. It was a sunny day, so we were flabbergasted when we saw the list of departing flights and the only one cancelled was ours. It turned out that it had struck something and the door was damaged. I am the last person who wants to fly on a plane that is not worthy; however, I was concerned about how I was going to get home. They started putting people on all kinds of flights just to get them back to the United States (such as Chicago and Boston). We did not want to go to either of these places. That turned out to be irrelevant since eventually all of the other flights were booked up and there was no option but to spend the night and catch a flight the next day. We did not want to go back to my brother's house. First, it was thirty minutes away, and second, he had already put us up for a long time! So we wanted to stay at one of the many hotels we could see from the airport. Unfortunately, all of them were booked up so we needed to go somewhere else.

The airlines found us a place at Euro Disney. Now all we had to do was get there! We were told to go up to the big red Disney bus and they would take us to the resort. When we approached the driver, he said that his bus did not provide that service. We needed to go to the upper level of our terminal, go to Door 36 and catch a bus to another terminal. From there we could catch the white Disney bus to the resort. So there we were hauling luggage once again all over the airport. We did find Door 36, but the instructions there for the bus were confusing. While waiting at the location that we hoped would bring about the correct bus, a man approached us and told us that he was a taxi driver and he could take us to the resort for the same price. Michele and I talked about it since it sounded too good to be true. We decided to do it but had second thoughts as this man took us to a very vacant parking garage and to a non-descript minivan and told us to get in. I asked to see his taxi license. He produced a document, but I realized that anyone could have created what he showed us on a home computer. Michele said she had a bad feeling about this, but I was dreading having to start this whole process again.

At this point we had been in the airport for about six hours. I just wanted to get to the resort and have some French wine! We decided to go with him. Our anxiety grew and grew, as we made our way through the countryside and through small villages. We did not know where we were, we couldn't read any of the signs, there were no billboards advertising for Disney, and we did not have a cell phone. I thought the airline people had said the trip was about twenty-five minutes, so when we were on the road for thirty minutes, I questioned the driver. He said it was close by. Another fifteen minutes went by and Michele and I were gripping each other tightly by the time we got there. We were so relieved. We apologized to the driver for our behavior and then went inside to get our room.

Unfortunately, the people at Euro Disney had no idea we were coming. We were the first of many to arrive and it became apparent that the airline did not make any financial commitments to Disney until everyone had arrived. So we sat there for a couple more hours waiting for everything to be hashed out. Another detail was that our daughter, and my mom who was watching her, were expecting us home that evening. We did not have a cell phone, laptop, or phone card, so we did not know what we were going to do to let them know what was going on. We finally asked one of the Disney employees if they would allow us to use their phone. They kindly did, so we made a quick call home. The details between the airline and Disney were finally ironed out, at which point we were able to get a nice meal and a good night sleep.

The next morning we got up, caught a bus to the airport, and arrived at the airline counter. The airline told us we were guaranteed a seat but refused to give us a seat assignment. Everyone else started boarding the plane, and we were afraid that we would have to wait another day. We were getting a little bit crazy by then. When they had boarded about two-thirds of the plane, they finally gave us seats. The airline did make good on their promises, but it was touch-and-go there for a while.

All Ends Well?

Now I don't want you to get any wrong ideas about our trip to Paris. Overall, we both had a phenomenal time in Paris. I can honestly say it was a high water mark in our relationship. Paris truly is a city for lovers.

Sadly, our traveling woes did not end there ... We flew back to Dulles, walked the half mile back to our car with our six pieces of luggage, and proceeded to drive home. We got lost at one point and ended up driving through Washington, DC. We got home a half hour later than we should have. To top it all off, we received a strange-looking letter in the mail about two weeks after our trip. It seemed that I had been speeding during our jaunt through downtown DC and had been picked up by one of the city's many speed cameras. Would the bleeding ever stop? I was beginning to think that our trip made a good sequel to *Planes, Trains and Automobiles*!

Chapter 30

Christmastime

Art: "The little lights... they aren't twinkling."
Clark: "I know, Art. Thanks for noticing."

from the movie "Christmas Vacation"

Loving our outdoor fun

Let the Transformation Begin

Ah yes! It is getting close to Christmas and you can feel that chill in the air. It is a time of great joy… and great anxiety. We always enjoy the holiday season and celebrate with many family traditions. We decorate the house from top to bottom, inside and out. We have 82 boxes and bags full of Christmas decorations. There are angels and Santa Clauses, wreaths and lights, reindeer and candles, garlands and lights, snowmen and snowflakes, bows and more lights, and of course, the stuffed animals! We have hundreds of stuffed animals donated by family and friends over the years. Our house becomes transformed during the Christmas season.

The first step of the decorating process is to drag all 82 boxes out of the basement and bring them upstairs. Then we go through all of them and decide which decorations will make the cut that year. There are always heated discussions between Michele and me as to which decorations we should just throw away. However, in the back of my mind, I am keeping them all in anticipation of giving some to our kids when they leave the nest and get a place of their own. All four of us then spend one entire day decorating the inside of the house. I have to admit that it looks quite nice once it is finished. It fills the house with a lot of Christmas cheer, and it leaves me brimming with Christmas spirit.

The outside of the house is my responsibility, and Ryan often lends me a hand with it now that he's gotten older. We line all of the bushes with lights, and we also set up illuminated angels, Santa Clauses, snowmen, and inflatable sculptures in the yard. We have a deer made of heavy gauge wire. He appears to be jumping, so we place him strategically where he seems to be jumping over a bush or some other obstacle in the yard. The reindeer used to be wrapped in lights, but one year half the lights cut out. For a while, I would troubleshoot the problem myself; ultimately, I ended up replacing each and every single bulb one at a time and checking all of the wiring to make sure there were no cuts. I didn't find any anything to cause the problem, so I had to make a decision. Should I re-wire the deer or consider this a lost cause? I seriously considered re-wiring him but then I asked myself if it really mattered. I decided that my time could be better spent doing something else.

Did I mention that we have lights, … lots and lots of lights? We also have numerous extension cords, timers, plug adapters, spotlights, special light hangers, power strips, and let's not forget the suction cups! Also, I built special little protective covers for all of the electrical connections so they wouldn't be in the rain causing short circuits of my masterpiece. Now, I am known in our community as the "Clark Griswald" of exterior illumination and have participated in community competitions (more on that later). I outlined the house with lights, which is kind of silly, since we live at the end of the last cul-de-sac in our neighborhood down a hill and surrounded by woods. I outlined the roof, the house itself, the garage, the doors, and all of the windows. I developed special hangers so I could have the lights travel along a brick archway we have over our front door. All strands of lights are on timers, so I don't have to go around plugging and unplugging everything every night. We must have close to twenty timers for the exterior illumination alone.

Allow Me to Describe the Adventure

It takes a solid day to set up the lights and it is quite an adventure. I am up on ladders as well as the roof itself. There is nothing like the anticipation of taking that first step onto the roof and hoping that the frost from the night before has melted. That sensation can be topped by the experience of standing on the roof in your winter jacket while the winds are whipping up around you. Of course, there is one area on our roof that really gives me the willies. It is along the peak of the roof right at the end by our wood stove chimney. I have to spend a lot of time right at the edge in order to outline the one side of the roof. The scary part is that it is about a forty-foot drop from this peak to the ground. I sometimes wonder if anyone inside would notice if I fell off the roof ... Anyway, I guess it is one of the hazards of being the Chief Master Outdoor Electrician. All kidding aside, I have to admit that the house looks nice when it is all done. I know others in the neighborhood appreciate all of the efforts since they will ask me where the lights are on those years I decide not to take the "roofline terror tour" and outline the house.

And Did I Say Competition?

I have to mention the one year we had a competition with our neighbors across the street. It started off well, but didn't end well. I cannot remember exactly how it started. Maybe it was during a conversation at their traditional Christmas Eve party. We probably stated that we had been the first in the neighborhood to put up our lights and they replied that they would be the last to take theirs down. It was then that we decided to have a friendly bet to see who would take down their house lights last. Well we both made it through January which proceeded into February and then all the way into March. The competition seemed to have no end in sight. (I was secretly hoping we could keep them up all year and I could just go right into the next Christmas season).

Little did I know that my plan would not come to fruition. Michele and I, along with our neighbors, just happened to be at a function with our priest, Father Nick. We somehow mentioned that we had this Christmas light competition going. You should have seen the look on his face! He couldn't believe what he had just heard, so he asked for clarification. When we told him again that our houses were still lit up from the previous Christmas, all of the blood ran out of his face. He reminded us that we were in the Lenten season where we were supposed to be fasting, praying, and giving of our time. He told us that Christmas lights should be turned off and removed from our houses immediately. They were. We decided to call it a draw.

Tree-Finding

Let's not forget the search for the perfect Christmas tree! Now, I have to start off by saying we actually have two full-size trees in our house. I am not really sure why. I guess when we were first married, we had an artificial tree and when we moved into a bigger house, we really wanted a live tree but did not want to give up the fake one—so we decided to have two. That's the best explanation I can come up with. Anyway, we started up the family tradition of going out to look for the perfect tree at the local tree farm. We would drive out to the farm, locate a tree, I would cut it down, and then we would bring it back to the house and spend the balance of the day decorating it. (For those of you keeping track, that's three full days of Christmas decorating).

Christmas tree shopping, a family adventure!

Now, my tree-finding philosophy is a bit different from the rest of my family's. When we find a tree that is a nice height and provides a nice view from all sides, I think we are done searching. Well, everyone else wants to continue and find a couple of trees that would suit our needs, which then leads to the conversation regarding which tree is best. I find this part of the experience a bit maddening. I remember one year, when my patience was running a bit thin, that I decided to change the experience. We got out of our car, we came across a tree that was nice, and I immediately cut it down. From the time we arrived to the time we left, it could not have been more than five minutes. On the drive home, I was happy as a clam while the rest of my family was in a state of shock. Suffice it to say that I never did that again.

A Lesson in Paying Attention

Now most excursions to find the perfect tree were pretty uneventful. Notice that I said "most." After cutting down a tree and getting it bound up, we then tie it to the top of the car. Typically, I am meticulous when it comes to securing things. My approach this one year, however, was a bit different. I am not sure if it was the eggnog or if we had an engagement that afternoon, but I must have rushed the tying down of the tree. As we were heading home, Danielle started to scream in the back seat about the tree. I was excited about the tree as well, but I did not see the need to be screaming. It was then that I realized she wasn't screaming about the tree but about how it was falling off the car. I immediately pulled over and did the job right the second time. This probably explains why that driver was flashing his lights at me. I have to pay more attention to what's going on around me!

Chapter 31

The Fat Lady is Singing

It Had to Happen Eventually

Well my friends, it had to happen sooner or later ... It was several years into my stay-at-home-dad experience when I realized I needed to get back into the workforce. There are only so many light bulbs you can change, and Michele's job was driving her to the edge of insanity. I took a long, hard look at what my skill set was and decided to give teaching a try. I knew I enjoyed working with youth in my coaching, religious education, various youth clubs, Boy Scouts, and substitute teaching experiences. To watch them mature and develop into young adults is an amazing event to witness. I believed I could be a positive part of that experience, so I decided to look into what it would take to become a teacher.

I did some research online and attended a workshop on what it takes to become a teacher in the "fast track" program. This program allows qualified professionals to bypass the usual method so they can get into the classroom more quickly. In other words, the school system needed math and science teachers, and they needed them badly. The first step in the process was to fill out the typical application. There was the resume and I had to track down my college transcripts, which was somewhat of a challenge. My SAT and GRE test scores from twenty-five years ago were also required. Thank goodness I have a decent filing system! Then I needed to find some good references who knew me personally as well as in a capacity to work with children. Finally, I needed to take a competency exam to make sure that I was qualified to teach specific math or science courses.

What am I saying Yes to?

After reviewing my transcripts from college and considering my work experience, the county asked me to consider becoming a physics teacher. At first, I was taken aback knowing that this is one of the hardest subjects in the high school curriculum. Then I sat down and really thought about it. It occurred to me that the students in any physics class would be top shelf, and therefore, I would probably have fewer problems with discipline. These students would also be focused. Beyond that, this career path was a way I could put all of my math and science skills to work while trying to make a positive impact on my students. I said yes and began to prepare. One of my first steps was to acquire some of the study guides to understand what knowledge was needed to do well on the test. The ***outline*** for the test was five pages long! A cold chill went up my spine as I looked at all of the topics covered including mechanics, electricity, magnetism, optics, waves, heat and thermodynamics, modern physics, atomic and nuclear structure, history and nature of science, science technology, and social perspectives.

I took physics back in high school as well as two courses at college. Many of the other courses I took at college were based on physics, but all of this educational experience was many years (actually decades) in my past. My work experience touched on physics, but I did not use the numerous theories and applications in my everyday work. I needed to begin studying so that I could become a better teacher. I began studying during the summer months of that year. I started to read my old textbook. It had to be some of the most boring reading I have ever done. It was difficult for me to stay focused on something so technical and dry. Without that focus, I wasn't really retaining all that much. It became apparent to me very early that I needed to go back to school to refresh myself. That way I would be able to take the required competency exam and do well.

I went back to school in the fall. It was exciting to be back in a classroom. Not only was I being educated (or should I say "re-educated?"), but I was getting to know my fellow classmates. I was obviously the oldest person in the class, but that was ok with me. I definitely brought a different perspective to the class. I was very anxious at the beginning and wasn't sure I had what it took to do well. The professor based the grade on tests, homework, and labs. The homework was the smallest percentage of the overall grade. I am pretty sure the professor just wanted to make sure we were doing problems outside of class to help us better understand the material. The labs were rather arduous. You would complete the lab work in the classroom and then go home and write up a two to six-page report. There was lots of reading and the preparation for the test was very time-consuming as well. I figured that I spent about twenty hours a week between going to class, doing homework, keeping up with the reading, preparing lab reports, and studying for tests. It was a challenge!

Testing Moments

The day of the first test finally came. It was a moment of truth. After finishing the test and reflecting on the experience, I had to laugh. I had a feeling that I had either done really well, or I had failed miserably. I found the experience to be a lot of fun and really enjoyed the format of the test. I thought that the examination really tested my knowledge of the subject, but it wasn't impossible. I waited a week for my grade. When it finally came, I was very pleased to see a 93% at the top. It appeared that I was on my way to trying to get an 'A.' I am happy to report that I did get an A in the class; it is an accomplishment that I am very proud of.

The competency exam was coming up, and I was still studying. My focus was now on the topics not covered in the class that I had just completed. This was about two-thirds of the material so I had my work cut out for me. I studied several hours a day for a couple of weeks and thought I should take a sample exam to see how well I was doing. Now before I go any further, I need to explain to you one of the grading policies of the test. The instructions for the test state that it is better to guess at an answer than to leave it blank. Well, the first practice test I took had twenty questions on it. The questions were all multiple choice with four choices each. I chuckled when I sat down realizing that I should get at least a '5' out of the 20 if I simply guessed. Well I took the test and got a '7.' I was shocked! I had put in countless hours throughout my life being exposed to physics and had studied over three hundred hours in the past several months and all I could get was a 7 out of 20?!? This was the first sample test I had taken and it dawned on me that: 1) the test was difficult, 2) the test was challenging to complete in the time allotted, 3) the equations for all of the problems had to be memorized, and 4) the test was difficult. I needed to put forth more effort and focus on the types of questions being asked in the sample test and start memorizing equations.

Once again I need to stop here and explain something to you ... there are a lot of equations. The class I took covered fourteen chapters from the textbook, and there were probably about fifty equations per chapter. That is about seven hundred equations, and that was only about one-third of the information to be covered on the test! I figure there were approximately 2,000 equations that need to be known for high school physics. To make matters worse, you need to have them memorized, but then understand what each variable in the equation stands for and what equation is used in what situation. I shut up and simply studied as much as I could since the test day was fast approaching. I finally felt a little more comfortable and decided to take a second practice exam. This one was seventy-five questions and I had ninety minutes to take the test. It was at this point that I began to scratch my head (again). I did a quick computation and determined that I had one minute and twelve seconds for each problem. Each problem was a short paragraph that you needed to read, comprehend, lay out, and solve. The anxiety meter went up another notch.

Test Anxiety Continues

This time the practice exam went a little smoother. I thought I understood what was being asked and had some of the equations memorized. I graded my answers and was horrified to learn that I got a 51%. This was better than just guessing, but not a whole lot better. I spent the next two days locked in my room memorizing things. Now you might think that I am a pushover, but most engineers don't go around memorizing things. We surround ourselves with lots of information and know where to go to get answers.
In fact, the professor for my physics course provided an equation sheet for each test, which is the way I think it should be done. It is my opinion that it is more important to understand the problem and know how to solve it than it is to memorize formulas. It has been my experience that when formulas are memorized, people just keep plugging numbers into various formulas until they get something to work. This is a poor strategy.

The day of the big test finally arrived. I have an admission ticket, my driver's license, five sharpened number 2 pencils and layered clothing. The ticket said that I must report to Smith Hall on the Towson University campus. There were no directions or instructions for parking, so I went on-line and looked them up on my own. No room number was given for Smith Hall, so I assumed that it was a small building. I arrived on campus. The first parking lot that I had identified had about five spots and they were all taken, so now I had to drive around since most parking on the college campus was permit only. I finally found parking and began to hike to Smith Hall. Smith Hall finally came into my view and it was five stories high and had the footprint of probably 1½ football fields. It was huge! So I am thinking to myself that it was no big deal. They'll probably have someone in the front lobby directing people taking the test to the proper classroom. I got into the lobby and looked around. There was no one there, and there were no signs telling us where to go. So what choice did I have but to begin wandering around the building until I finally saw a line forming outside of a lecture hall. I thought to myself that this had to be it. I asked those in line if they were taking the exam and they stated that they were.

After waiting in line for a couple of minutes, someone stopped by and asked if we were taking the exam. When we stated that we were, she told us to follow her. We went up two floors and waited in another line. After about 10 minutes, I handed my admission ticket and driver's license to the proctor and was told I was in the wrong place. I was to report to the first place I had stopped! I went back there and finally checked in and got a seat. I proceeded to get myself situated in the very last row of the class. It turned out that the forty to fifty people in the room were not all taking the Physics competency exam. There were people taking the exam for English and others were taking it for Social Studies or Math or Special Needs. I thought this was interesting, and I also surmised it was a good way to ensure no cheating occurred.

Lots of Testing Rules

The rules for the test were then reviewed. For instance, the issue of the specific people who were allowed to use calculators was discussed. Everyone was allowed to use a calculator ... except those taking the physics exam. I found this ironic since those of us taking the physics exam would be taking a test that would probably consist of 70% computational problems. (In fact, I was flabbergasted when I learned on one of the practice exams, that they expected us to know what the "sine of 60 degrees" was)! Anyway, the proctors then proceeded to hand out the tests to each respective group. The last group to be called was Physics, and when they asked us to raise our hands, I was the only one. Everyone in the class slowly turned around to look at me as if to say, "What moron would be silly enough to take a Physics competency exam?" Apparently, that was me.

I took the exam, and it was brutal. I took every second of the 120 minutes to complete all one hundred problems. The person taking the test next to me stopped about half-way through and eventually put his head down on the desk. I was thinking to myself that he must have really screwed up and had not properly prepared himself for the test. When the test was over, I thought I would reach out to him. I asked him how he thought he had done. He replied that he thought he had done fine. He shared with me that he had finished early and thought many others taking various tests had as well. Oh, if I had only been so lucky...

Chapter 32

No Regrets

"I'm home again
I see my wife,
Little boy,
Little girl...
Hello world"
- *Lady Antebellum*

Fond Reflections

Looking back, it has been a wild ride. I wonder about how I will feel when I look back on this time in my life years from now and whether or not I will have any regrets. I can honestly say that I believe that I will not. I honestly tried to make good use of the time I had. I tried to be productive. I tried to make the world a better place for my family, my neighbors, and the greater community. It is funny to look back and remember when I started on this journey. I realize that there was irony in working forty hours a week while making money, and then retiring to work sixteen-hour days, seven days a week, and receiving no pay. Even though there were trials and tribulations, there were tremendous rewards, insights, and revelations. I learned that the best experiences were the ones involving relationships. Here are some of the highlights of my years as a stay-at-home dad:

Lock and Load - I love all of my godchildren. They are all unique and possess many endearing qualities. I wish I could have spent more time with each of them, but I do have many great memories of the time I did spend with them. One of my fondest memories is when I visited my best friend Doug from my high school years. He now has a beautiful wife and three wonderful children, one of which is my goddaughter. I love interacting with all three of the kids, so I look for opportunities to do things with them. You can imagine my joy when I discovered that they had a Nerf machine gun, complete with a stand to mount the mammoth gun on. They actually had a number of these styrofoam-bullet guns, but the machine gun was by far the biggest and baddest. We had many gun wars that weekend and laughed as we shot at each other from across the room.

That Monday they went off to school and I got an evil idea. I loaded the smaller Nerf guns and left them outside in the garage. At the end of the hallway leading to the garage, I set up the machine gun. It took an hour or so to prepare for this epic battle, but it was worth every minute. I heard the garage door open and the kids pile out of the car. There was a moment of silence. I suppose they were pondering why their Nerf guns were out in the garage. It must not have taken long for them to figure it out as the three of them came bursting into the hallway with guns blazing. That is when I opened fire with the machine gun. There were bullets so thick in the air that it was getting hard to breathe. The battle lasted for several minutes, and when the air cleared, I realized we had created a memory.

This realization proved to be true about three months later when Ryan and I were in that part of the country visiting colleges. We planned it so we could use their house as a home base. I had purchased a couple of Nerf guns and extra ammo clips and ammo belts. When we arrived, there was a note on the door telling us to be cautious as we entered. Ryan and I entered the room carefully, but were immediately barraged with a volley of bullets rarely witnessed during the course of human history. It was brutally fun!

Look out, I'm a mean shot!

Pinch Me - My brother has persevered through some challenging times. His patience and fortitude have paid off, and he has a very successful career that landed him in Paris with his wife and two beautiful children. Both of his children are my godchildren and I love them very much. Anyway, my parents would visit my brother and his family about twice a year. They would typically ask me to go, but since money was always a bit tight, I would politely say I could not. They really wanted me to come see my brother and his family, so they offered to pay for my flight. I couldn't refuse this once-in-a-lifetime offer, so I went. Paris was simply amazing! I walked around the beautiful city all day long meeting my parents at various museums and sites throughout the day.

In the evening we would all sit around enjoying each other's company over a couple of glasses (or was it bottles?!?) of wine. It was one of those special moments, and we all realized it even at that time. After hours of conversation, we realized that we had to go to bed. It was very late. I remember very clearly going to bed that first night. I got into my pajamas, slipped under the covers, and put my head down on the pillow. The bed was right underneath the only window in the room. I looked out the window and it framed the Eiffel Tower perfectly. I kept waiting for the dream to end, but I realized that I was just tremendously blessed.

Your Most Endearing Quality Is... - Michele and I have been involved in Marriage Encounter for over twenty years. It is a wonderful organization that provides "tune up" services for marriages just like you do for a car. When people ask us what it is all about, we say that it takes good marriages and makes them great. Anyway, one of the many tools we learned through Marriage Encounter is one called the affirmation exercise. This is an exercise in which someone is selected from the group of people and everyone else in the group says something that they appreciate about that person. This exercise can be done individually for specific people or done for everyone in the group. It is a very powerful experience since you do not know what people's perception of you is until they say it out loud in front of others. Anyway, Michele and I decided that we could apply this to our family as well. We found that the perfect time to do this is when we are driving somewhere. We would tell the kids we were doing the exercise and give them a couple of minutes to collect their thoughts. Then we would pick someone and each person would say what they appreciated about that person. Then we would do the same thing for the next person and so on until all four of us had gone through the exercise. It has been a highlight for me over the past seven years since I probably value the opinion of no one more than that of my family.

Time, Talent or Treasure - The saying at our church is you can give your time, talent, or treasure as a gift to the church in order for it to strive and meet its goals. Since I had quit my job, the treasure chests were a bit low, so I had to look to the other areas in my life to meet my obligation to make the world a better place. I volunteered in our church and the local community for thousands of hours. Some of it was grueling and very challenging. Some of it was unproductive and a total waste of my time. Some of it was rewarding beyond words. One type of outreach that I did, which lacked the response I had anticipated, was reaching out to those in need. Close friends would suffer through a difficult disease or lose a loved one. I wanted to call them or visit them to make sure they were all right. I had the time and they were suffering. It seemed very logical to me. I suppose that I would want someone to do the same for me. What I did not expect was the response to my simple actions. People were genuinely appreciative. They would keep thanking me, which just made me feel embarrassed. But then it struck me as to why they responded the way that they did: They knew that there was nothing in it for me. I had no hidden agenda. I was there because I wanted to be, and God had given me the opportunity.

The Smell of Musty Magazines - As you have probably already gathered, I love magazines. I know it sounds weird, but I like the feel of the pages whether they are crisp and new, or faded and worn. I love the sound of the pages turning. I love what is written on the pages. They contain specific information about your particular area of interest. There is a musty smell to an old magazine that I like and can spot readily. I probably like it because it tells me that a magazine is close by. I have collected magazines for decades, specifically ones dealing with cars and, even more specifically, ones dealing with muscle cars. Over the years, I bought a lot of magazines from a particular used car magazine dealer. The dealer was a married couple whose names were Dave and Carol. When Dave died of cancer, I continued to support Carol and her business by buying magazines at least once a year. I would drive to her house, which was about forty-five minutes from where I lived, to pick up the magazines. We started learning more about each other and became friends. Her son lives overseas, so I would offer to help her with anything she needed to have done around the house. Sometimes she took me up on my offer and other times she didn't. She started talking to me about how she wanted to sell her business. It was a significant collection that filled a two-story barn, her garage, and her basement. I said I was interested but could not possibly take the entire business, since I did not have the money and I felt the space requirements were more than I had. She eventually had several people interested in purchasing the business but wanted to know exactly what she had. I told her I would help her quantify all the magazines she had. For the next several months, I came to her house and helped her count all of the magazines. It was hard and sometimes dirty work, but I was in heaven since I was up to my eyeballs in magazines! I am happy to say that she did eventually sell the business. I am happier to say that we are still good friends today.

Hey Bro - I love to work with my hands. It is fun for me to put forth honest effort and then be able to step back when I am finished and admire my work. My hardscaping business through which I built retaining walls, patios, walkways, and steps put my skills to the test and provided me with great satisfaction. I have been able to work for some great people and build some wonderful projects. One of the unexpected benefits was to be able to work with my brother-in-law, David, who is a brick mason. I was always on the lookout for opportunities to work together and put his extraordinary skills to good use. Over the years, we have worked together many times. We kid around, give each other a hard time, and just have a good time hanging around each other. It has been a real pleasure to spend some quality time with him.

Help! - I have taken a number of personality tests over the years. I always like to think that I am a "helper" type personality, but I almost always come out as an "organizer." My stay-at-home dad experience has allowed me to become more of a helper and I have enjoyed it tremendously. My parents live in a single family house. They are getting older and I have watched over the years as it has become more and more difficult for them to keep up with the maintenance and upkeep of their house. One example is when they told me how the shelves in their closets had fallen down shortly after they had moved into the house. They had called the builder who had a crew come out and put the shelving back up. I was a bit surprised that this should happen in a house that was just built. I was even more surprised when it happened a second time! When it happened a third time, I told them not to contact the builder and that I would come to reinstall them myself. When I came out, I was shocked to find that they were attaching the shelving bracket to the drywall, but not into the studs! In my opinion this is simple Carpentry 101. In about a day and half's work, I had rebuilt all of the closet shelving in the entire house. This led to me helping out with a variety of other tasks around their house during a week in the summer and eventually a week in the winter as well. I got the feeling of satisfaction from completing the numerous projects. A larger benefit was being able to help my parents. The greatest benefit of all was spending time with my parents. Once again, I had been provided this great opportunity, and I was pleased I had taken advantage of it.

Leave Me Alone! - We live in a great neighborhood. We know almost everyone in the neighborhood and get along well with them. They have become very close friends and even more so since I became a stay-at-home dad. I have helped many out when they have been between a rock and a hard place. I have helped them maintain their houses. I have been able to have fun with them. There have been the parties, the dinners, the happy hours, and the leaf wars.

You read correctly. I said, "leaf wars." Allow me to explain: Our neighbor lives across the street in a beautiful two-story Victorian house. They have three wonderful daughters. They take great pride in their lawn. They shared with me that one of the main reasons they picked the lot they built their house on was the fact that there were so few trees. You see, they had a bad experience with a wooded lot sometime in their past. Our lot, on the other hand, is covered in trees. Unfortunately for them, the winds blow during the autumn season from our lawn to theirs so no matter how much I rake our lawn, there are leaves that blow from our lawn to theirs. They would jokingly remind us of this fact. We, of course, would deny it. The "leaf wars" started off as only the exchange of words and then it grew into more physical acts. There were the cartoons clipped out of the Sunday paper with references to raking leaves. Then there was the exchange of silly notes. We received a gift-wrapped box of leaves and a badminton racquet covered with leaves (that one was a bit strange)! The hanging pot full of leaves on a pole about eight-feet-high in their front yard was pretty creative. Then it really escalated, and I filled over thirty garbage bags full of leaves, and under the cover of darkness, we dragged them over to their house and placed them in front of their front door. I accidentally pushed the screen out of the frame of the door. I felt so guilty about it that I called them the next day to make sure their door was ok. (Of course, I did not mention the leaves). When the wife did not admit to anything being wrong, I actually became afraid. I knew there was a retaliation to come, and I was right.

About two weeks later, Ryan called me from the top of the driveway on his way out to the school bus. He said I needed to come outside to check out our driveway right away. When I did, I was shocked to see a stack of leaf-filled garbage bags about six feet high blocking our driveway. I spent the rest of the day removing the bags. That is when a truce was called. We decided to scale back our efforts. This was becoming too labor-intensive, but it was fun!

Take Me Away - Sometimes we find places in our lives where it feels close to perfect. This happened to Michele and me on a Caribbean cruise we took. One night we came across a piano bar. We sat down to have some cocktails and just enjoy each other's company. The piano player was excellent. He not only played piano very well, but he had an outstanding repertoire of songs which he sung very well. He interacted with his audience and drew us all into the experience of that moment. We all sat there singing songs that had inspired us over the years and were figuratively taken to another place. Before we knew it, several hours had passed and it was time to go to bed. Michele and I found ourselves back there the next night having just as good a time. It was a little slice of heaven here on earth.

On Your Mark...- I love cars, and the faster the better. Michele once suggested that I purchase a new Chevrolet Camaro that I had been drooling over for years. I was a bit surprised at her suggestion, but not silly enough to question it! I went out searching for a good car and came across a 2002 Chevrolet Camaro SS with modifications by SLP. It was beautiful. It was black with leather interior, T-tops, and a really nice sound system. It was by far the best car I had ever owned. The car packed a whopping 345 horsepower which was pretty high for a stock car at the time. Driving it was a dream. It was a six speed and ran with ferocity! The car looked mean and ran mean. It was extraordinary! It had always been a dream of mine to go drag racing. I had gone to many drag races but had never participated. I decided I had to give it a try. I took Ryan with me so he could be there to experience my dream as well. According to car test magazines, the car was capable of 100 miles per hour and could dip down into the 13-second range. My first run was a bit disappointing. I ran at 98.4 miles per hour at a time of 14.4 seconds. It was my first drag-racing experience, so I was really trying to get a feel for how it was done. The second run was bit more promising. I did not drop down into the 13's, but I did crack the 100 mile-per-hour barrier. I wanted to give it another try, but Ryan was freezing to death in the grandstands so we called it a night. Overall, it was a thrilling experience!

Picasso Move Aside - Danielle is the artist of the family. She loves to sing, work in the local play productions, and create beautiful artwork in the various classes she participates in. She loves to help you pick out what clothes you are buying or what you are going to wear that day. I have to say that she is very good at it. So when it came time to do a minor remodeling of our kitchen, I thought that it would be a wonderful opportunity to tap into her natural skills and work together. We went to the local hardware store and picked out new knobs for the cabinets as well as paint for the walls. We stopped by the cloth shop to pick up material to reupholster the kitchen seats. She helped pick out the tile for the new floors as well as the tiles for the kitchen counter backsplash. Then she helped with various aspects of the implementation of the new palette for the kitchen. In the end it turned out beautifully, and she had experienced what it was like to do some remodeling. The greatest benefit was that I got to experience some quality time with my wonderful daughter.

Quality time with Danielle

I'll Give You A Drawing - It is fun to celebrate when someone you know well has a success. In that moment I find that I am not only having a great time, but reflecting on all of the effort along the way to culminate in the celebration of the success. This was especially true when I reflect on the journey of my brother.

First I need to provide some background ... My brother Chris has been drawing since he was about five years old. I clearly remember that almost every day after dinner he would go to his bedroom and draw for an hour or so. He had a genuine talent from day one. He had champions along the way like Mrs. Tilghman, his first grade teacher. She saw his potential and suggested to my parents that they consider lessons for him. They did some research, found a teacher, and Chris took lessons for a couple of years. He kept drawing through elementary school, middle school, and high school. Then he wanted to go onto college and major in illustration. Looking back on this, I have to say that my parents were taking somewhat of risk in a major such as this. They truly believed in my brother and sent him off to school. He graduated and lived in Hoboken, New Jersey for several years while pursuing his dream of being a comic book artist. There were some lean times along the way when he was cutting his own hair and eating a lot of hot dogs, but he persevered. He did some work for his fellow classmates, and even worked for me in the engineering firm I was associated with at the time.

Eventually his dream became a reality, and he produced numerous comic books for the big names like Marvel and DC Comics. He even got to illustrate one of his favorite superheroes, Batman. His career changed gears, and he got into some advertising and then did some computer-animated television shows. Up to this point he had been independent and had not really had "steady" employment with one employer. That changed when he began working on movies. First there was *Robots* in which he helped develop various scenes in the movie. In *Ice Age 2 Meltdown,* he played a larger role and had his first directing experience in the animated short film featuring Scrat, the lovable pre-historic squirrel who will do anything for his acorn. Chris got an Oscar nomination for his efforts on this very funny short. That's when he looked for an opportunity to direct a full-length animated film. He found that opportunity in the film *Despicable Me.* It took two years to develop the film. When it came time for its release, Chris was very conservative and did not want to predict any large success.

The film was phenomenally successful and went on to gross over a quarter of a billion dollars here in the United States and even more overseas. He was proud of his work but very modest. He always played it conservative and did not brag about how well he thought the movie would do. He treated it as a job. He also made sure that his family was involved in this phenomenal event in his life. There are even references to his children in the film! When the decision to have a premiere was made, Chris decided to invite our parents, his wife's parents, his wife's sister and fiancé, as well as our family. Danielle could not attend since she was part of a play in our hometown and Michele stayed home to take care of her.

The event was held on a beautiful sunny LA day at the Nokia Theater. It started off with a "red carpet" event. (Note: there was no red carpet. It was a yellow carpet instead since the minions in the movie were primarily yellow). It was amazing when we got to see the actors who provided the voices for the various characters. The biggest thrill for Ryan was seeing Steve Carell and actually talking to him briefly and getting his autograph. My biggest thrill was seeing Julie Andrews. I love her because of her work on one of the greatest films of all time, *The Sound of Music*. We watched the movie after the "yellow carpet" experience. I found myself crying at times realizing how hard Chris had worked to get to this point and how proud I was of his accomplishment. The film was then followed by a big party. I made sure to take pictures of the actors that Danielle liked and even got a photograph from Elise Fisher who played the voice of Agnes. Chris hobnobbed with the big names that were there, but always made time to come back and hang out with his family as well. That was actually the best part of the experience for me ... realizing that his primary value was family.

Pop Pop's Masons?!?- Pop Pop Derlunas is somewhat of a legend in our family. As Michele's dad, he was sort of the person I was measuring up to during our years of courtship and even into our marriage. His ability to keep a cool head under pressure and his endless support of us throughout our marriage were simply inspiring and there was no way

I could possibly repay him for all he did for us. When he passed away in the spring of 2008 after battling cancer, it was like the wind went out of all of our sails. He was the "glue" in our family, seeing everyone through the tough times and being there to celebrate in the good times. In ways he was Michele's best friend. We all had a tough time coming to terms with the fact that he was gone. So when the opportunity came up to put together a team for the American Cancer Society's Relay for Life program, we decided to do it as a family. We made Danielle, who was about thirteen at the time, our team captain. We collected contributions and then attended the event. We walked laps around the track in his honor and burned a luminary in his memory. It was a moving experience and to do it as a family made it even more memorable and special.

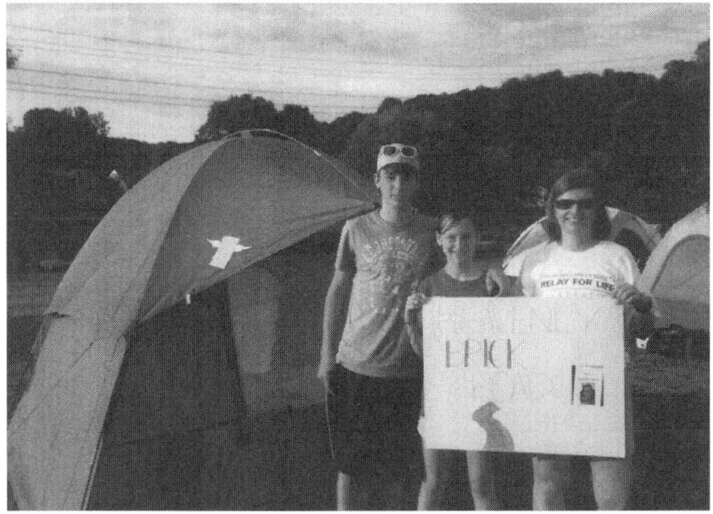

Participating in Relay for Life for Pop Pop Derlunas

I Love You - I love all of my family and they mean the world to me. I sometimes tell them that I would take a bullet for them and I mean it. So it hurt a little bit when Ryan began to pull away from us as a family, and he and I did not get along as well as we did when he was younger. I was happy that he was becoming independent and I understood that there were now two men in the house and that we were bound to butt heads once in a while. Either way, it was still a bit painful. So when he came into our bedroom one evening and asked to speak with me, I was not sure what to expect. He took me back to his bedroom, and when he turned to face me, he had tears in his eyes. It was then that I began to worry. It turned out that I had nothing to worry about. He told me that he loved me very much and then gave me a big hug. He went on to explain how a friend of his was having some serious troubles with his father. Through his friend's experience, Ryan came to realize how special our relationship was. It is a moment that I will treasure forever.

I have always believed that time is the most precious gift that we have to give to others. My experience as a stay-at-home dad proved that to me time and again.

Appendix

Afterward

Well, about a year has gone by since I stopped being "Mr. Mom." It turns out that the teaching thing did not pan out. I interviewed with the county Board of Education and my gut reaction is that the interview went well. However, the county decided to actually let teachers go that year and didn't hire anyone for the fast track program in math and sciences for which I had interviewed. I had been simultaneously pursuing getting back into civil engineering. I had not put much faith in landing an engineering position since there were few to be found. (You would think with all of the stimulus monies being spent by the federal government, a lot of which was spent on infrastructure, that it would help civil engineers. In reality, the money was spent on projects that were "on the shelf," so there was a large benefit to the contractors and very little benefit to civil engineers). In addition, I hadn't practiced any substantive engineering in the seven years that I was a stay-at-home dad. I interviewed for a job with the local Department of Transportation. When I found out that over twenty people had applied for the position, I laughed and thought to myself that there was no way I would get the job. Two weeks later they made me an offer. Since the reason for interviewing was to find a job, I took it. It struck me once again how the Lord works in mysterious ways. I have been back at work for a while now. To be honest I could write a book on my experience there. That will just have to wait for another time ...

My stay-at-home dad experience taught me a lot. I learned that there are a lot of good things to do in the world. I am glad that I got to experience trying to make the world a better place. I learned that I can think on my own. This mentality was sharpened in the development and maintenance of my two small businesses. I was able to apply this trait to my current job, and I have been trying to make a positive difference there. I learned that I love to be outdoors. Now I appreciate when I am outdoors even more. I learned how wonderful it feels to be in good shape. Now I strive to take better care of myself. I love my family more than anything in the world. I truly would sacrifice anything for them.

I couldn't ask for more. I have always had the philosophy that if I were to die today, I would die a happy man. I have always tried to put forth my best effort and I have had a blessed life. I cannot wait to see what the future holds!

Acknowledgments

There are so many people I would like to thank for helping me and inspiring me to write this book. First, I would like to thank Mom and Dad who have always believed in me. They have been very patient and have stood by me through thick and thin. They have been great role models on what it means to be a good parent and to be happily married. Obviously the Boy Scouting program has played a large role in my life. Mr. Butler, who was my Scoutmaster when I was a boy, was truly a mentor for me. He showed me many new skills and presented me with numerous opportunities. My only hope is that I can have an impact on just one boy half as large as the impact that he has had on my life. I also need to mention the numerous scouts I have worked with over the years. It has been my privilege and honor, and my life has been changed because of the roles that each of you have played in my life. My teachers over the years have also been strong mentors in my life. There are many that come to mind; however, Mr. Smith, who was my 10th Grade Biology teacher, saw something in me that others did not. He also told me it was ok to laugh and to have a good time. I would be remiss if I did not mention the book 32 Third Graders and One Class Bunny written by Phillip Done. This book was an inspiration to me not only from a teaching perspective, but also in showing how a book could be written to be both funny and inspiring. I have to mention my counselor who truly inspired me to finish this book and get it published. My brother Chris was instrumental by providing a couple of "drawrings" for the book. Also, I need to thank Lauraine Everson for doing the cover art. I have to mention the support of my family, especially to Michele and Ryan, for helping out with the editing. I couldn't have done it without your support! Jean Marx has been instrumental in getting this book to publication. I couldn't have done it without her. Finally, I would like to thank all of the people in our community who have shown interest in my book. I feel truly blessed to have so many wonderful people in my life!

About the Author

Jim has spent his entire life living on the East Coast and currently resides in Parkton, Maryland, a town north of Baltimore. He is married to his wonderful wife Michele and has two children, Ryan and Danielle. Besides tinkering with cars, you can find him working in the yard or spending time with his family. He has always been inspired by "slice of life" movies and stories. Therefore, it only made sense that he write down some of his experiences while being a stay-at-home dad, or what he fondly calls his "Mr. Mom" experience. Some of these stories are funny, which goes to prove that there is nothing funnier than real life. Other stories are inspirational as Jim discovers the amazing spirit found in those around us. Jim truly believes that his life has been a blessing and is thankful each day. He hopes that this book puts a smile on your face and touches your heart.

7571486R00179

Made in the USA
San Bernardino, CA
10 January 2014